Laugh Your Way to Health & Wealth

Compiled by:

Ben Brooks

&

Tom Hopkins

Laugh Your Way to Health and Wealth
FIRST EDITION
Copyright 2006 by
Tom Hopkins International, Inc. and Ben Brooks & Associates
7531 E. 2nd Street   4425 N. 24th Street, #125
Scottsdale, AZ 85251   Phoenix, AZ 85016
800-528-0446   602-264-1565
www.tomhopkins.com   www.benbrooks.com

Printed in the United States of America.
ISBN: 0-938636-53-7

Library of Congress Cataloging in Publication Data
Hopkint, Tom and Brooks, Ben
Laugh your way to health and wealth.

Originally published: Scottsdale, Ariz.: Tom Hopkins
International, Inc. c2006
Includes index.

CONTENTS

Some very funny stuff!

The jokes were originally put together according to category but reading the same type of joke one after another became 'unfunny.' So, the jokes are now in random order.

An index is provided on page 150 in case you are seeking a particular type of joke.

Mark your favorite jokes with a highlighter or flags for ease of locating them when an appropriate situation arises...that is, until you have them memorized from sharing them so much!

We hope you enjoy reading them as much as we have enjoyed laughing over them.

DEDICATION

To my many wonderful family members, friends, and associates who have enriched my life over the years...especially those who have stood by me and helped me attain my goals. Particular acknowledgment to my loved ones Tres, Julie, Bruck, Haley and Lovisha, and to my trusted confidant, colleague and friend, Michael Sawhill. Thanks for all of the support. May you always find laughter in your lives.

Ben **B**rooks

To the three million students who have allowed me the privilege of training them to be the best they can be in the honorable profession of sales. Thank you for appreciating the power of humor in the art and science of selling.

Tom **H**opkins

Introduction

"Did you hear the one about..." is often how Tom Hopkins and Ben Brooks begin their conversations, and gales of laughter can usually be heard once the punch line is delivered. Tom and Ben love to share not only the memories, experiences and good times of their very long friendship but also the best new jokes as they both believe in the power of using humor both in friendship and business.

Tom Hopkins, the world's leading sales trainer and Ben Brooks, the unchallenged leader in investing and developing real estate, have been friends for over 30 years. When they met during a presentation Tom made to the Phoenix Board of Realtors in 1975, they did not realize just how much they had in common.

Both men had a rather rough start in the business-world. Tom quit college after three months, got married at 19, had a child by 20 and started working in construction. He decided that there had to be an easier way to earn a living, so he studied for his real estate license. On the third try, he passed the exam and began selling real estate.

Ben never considered college because he was working several jobs to try to support his single mother, sister and brother. He married at 21 and had his first child by 22. He also decided to sell real estate, hoping it would be a good way to make a living for his family. Both men learned their crafts through hard work and persistence. There were lots of ups and downs on their way to success. One of the most important attributes they shared, however, was that they retained their ability to enjoy humor throughout their challenging starts.

Tom and Ben still have a lot in common! Both are very accomplished businessmen. Both started their own businesses relatively early in their careers. And both believe that humor is one of the critical keys to leading a happy life, bettering your health *and* increasing your wealth!

In fact, humor has been proven to better one's health. It reduces stress, lowers blood pressure, boosts the immune system, improves the brain functionality, and even helps protect the heart. Renowned writer, Norman Cousins was one of the first to study this concept. After years of study and focusing on healing himself from both a bout of cancer and heart problems, he said, "Laughter is a form of internal jogging. It moves your internal organs around. It enhances respiration. It is an igniter of great expectations."

Humor also helps in reducing pain because it takes peoples' minds off their ailments. It's a fact that happy people are generally healthier people!

Laughter is also important in relationships. It can help start new relationships, strengthen existing ones and break down barriers in those that might be strained. There's nothing better than sharing a good laugh with a close friend or relative.

Humor is also very effective in business. Tom uses humor in all of his educational sales seminars. He feels that if his students laugh, they are more likely to remember the message because they're having fun. They will have lowered their mental barriers to traditional learning. If someone is expecting a good laugh, they're more attentive and open…waiting for the joy that humor brings.

Ben also uses humor effectively in business. He has an impeccable sense of timing and knows when and where to throw in some humor or a good joke. He also uses humor whenever he is giving a speech, doing a seminar or marketing his company. Ben knows that clients and customers are more likely to want to work with someone they truly enjoy being around.

Both Tom and Ben agree to "Take your business seriously…but not necessarily yourself!" A good sense of humor is crucial with subordinates, customers, associates, employees and the public. Take caution, though, timing is critical!! You certainly do not want to offend anyone with untimely humor because it could have a very negative effect.

Tom and Ben have shared years of laughter and fun. They have both collected jokes for decades and have teamed together to compile some of their favorites that can be used in the personal and/or business setting. Whether you need a joke to open a meeting, use at a client dinner or close a sales call, you will find some funny material in this book. Hopefully, these jokes will assist you in having some laughs in your life, bettering your health and growing your wealth.

KEY

🕷 = Animals

? = Blonde

☺ = Children

✚ = Doctor/Medical

⧗ = Elderly

◼ = Ethnic

⛳ = Golf

🏛 = Lawyer

☯ = Male/Female Relationships

✳ = Miscellaneous

🚓 = Police

○ = Religious

♟ = Sales/Business

✈ = Travel

❋ **A** pirate walked into a bar and the bartender said, *"Hey, I haven't seen you in a while. What happened? You look terrible!"*

"What do you mean?" said the pirate, *"I feel fine."*

"What about the wooden leg? You didn't have that before."

"Well, we were in a battle and I got hit with a cannon ball, but I'm fine now."

"Well, okay, but what about that hook? What happened to your hand?"

"We were in another battle. I boarded a ship and got into a sword fight. My hand was cut off. I got fitted with a hook. I'm fine, really."

"What about that eye patch?"

"Oh, one day we were at sea and a flock of birds flew over. I looked up and one of them did his business right in my eye."

"You're kidding," said the bartender, *"you couldn't lose an eye just from that!"*

"It was the first day with the hook."

⧗ **D**id you hear about the old couple that died at the drive-in theater?

They went to see "Closed for the Winter."

☺ **A** mother invited some people to dinner. At the table, she turned to their six-year-old daughter and said, *"Would you like to say the blessing?"*

"I wouldn't know what to say," the girl replied.

"Just say what you hear Mommy say."

The daughter bowed her head and said, *"O, Lord, why on earth did I invite all these people to dinner?"*

☯ **A** man and his wife entered the dentist's office.

"I want a tooth pulled," the man said. *"We're in a big hurry, so let's not fool around with gas or Novocain or any of that stuff."*

"You are a very brave man," remarked the dentist. *"Which tooth is it?"*

The man turned to his wife and said, *"Show him your bad tooth Honey."*

⛳ **G**olfer: *"I'd move heaven and earth to be able to break 100 on this course."*

Caddy: *"Try heaven. You've already moved most of the earth."*

Paddy O'Sullivan was driving down the street in a sweat because he had an important meeting and couldn't find a parking place.

Looking up to heaven he said, *"Lord, take pity on me. If you find me a parking place I will go to Mass every Sunday for the rest of me life and give up me Irish Whiskey."*

Miraculously, a parking place appeared.

Paddy looked up again and said, *"Never mind, I found one."*

A husband looking through the paper came upon a study that said women use more words than men. Excited to prove to his wife that he had been right all along when he accused her of talking too much, he showed her the study results.

It read: *"Men use about 15,000 words per day but women use 30,000."*

The wife thought about it for a while, then finally she said, *"It is because we have to repeat everything we say."*

The husband said *"What?"*

☺ The children were lined up in the cafeteria of a Catholic elementary school for lunch. At the head of the table was a large pile of apples.

The nun made a note, and posted on the apple tray: *"Take only ONE. God is watching."*

Moving further along the lunch line, at the other end of the table was a large pile of chocolate chip cookies.

A child had written a note, *"Take all you want. God is watching the apples."*

⌛ Three elderly holy men were asked: *"When you're in the casket, and friends, family and congregants are mourning over you, what would you like to hear them say?"*

Episcopal Priest: *"I would like to hear them say that I was a wonderful husband, a fine spiritual leader, and a great family man."*

Catholic Priest: *"I would like to hear that I was a wonderful teacher and a servant of God who made a huge difference in people's lives."*

Rabbi: *"I would like to hear them say, 'Look, he's moving!'"*

✳ **A** blind man is walking along the sidewalk with his dog when all of a sudden the dog leads him right off the end of a curb. He falls to his knees and scratches himself up pretty good. With that, he staggers to his feet, reaches in his pocket, gets a dog biscuit and starts calling for the dog.

An observer goes over to the blind man and asks, *"I just saw your dog lead you off the end of a curb and I am curious why you are trying to give him a dog biscuit as a reward?"*

The blind man says, *"I'm not trying to reward him! I'm just trying to find out where his head is so I can kick his butt!"*

■ **O**le died. So Lena went to the local paper to put a notice in the Obituaries. The gentleman at the counter, after offering his condolences, asked Lena what she would like to say about Ole.

Lena replied, *"You just put 'Ole died'."*

The gentleman, somewhat perplexed, said, *"That's it? Just 'Ole died?' Surely, there must be something more you'd like to say about Ole. If it's money you're concerned about, the first five words are free. We must say something more."*

So Lena pondered for a few minutes and finally said, *"O.K. You put, Ole died. Boat for sale."*

🕷 **A** burglar broke into a house one night. He shined his flashlight around, looking for valuables. When he picked up a CD player to place it in his sack, a strange, disembodied voice echoed from the dark saying, *"Jesus is watching you."*

He nearly jumped out of his skin, clicked his flashlight out, and froze. When he heard nothing else, he shook his head, promised himself a vacation after the next big score, then clicked the light on and began searching for more valuables.

Just as he pulled the stereo out so he could disconnect the wires, clear as a bell he heard, *"Jesus is watching you."*

Freaked out, he shone the light around frantically, looking for the source of the voice. Finally, in the corner of the room his flashlight beam came to rest on a parrot.

"Did you say that?" he hissed at the parrot.

"Yep," the parrot confessed then, squawked, *"I'm just trying to warn you."*

The burglar relaxed. *"Warn me, huh? Who in the world are you?"*

"Moses," replied the bird.

"Moses?" the burglar laughed. *"What kind of people would name a parrot Moses?"*

The parrot replied, *"The same kind who would name a Rottweiler Jesus."*

🕷 **T**his cowboy goes into a bar and orders two fingers of whiskey. He's sitting there sipping his shot, looks in the back and sees a poker game going on. He sees a dog in one of the chairs and asks the bartender, *"Is that a dog sitting in there playing poker?"*

The bartender says, *"Yes, he's in here every day playing poker."*

The guy says, *"Every day? That's really something! He must be really good."*

The bartender replies, *"Nope, he can't play a lick."*

The cowboy says, *"Can't play a lick and he's in here playing every day? What's the problem?"*

The bartender says, *"Well, every time he gets a good hand, he wags his tail."*

🏆 An employer asked a candidate, *"Young man, do you think you can handle a variety of work?"*

"I ought to be able to. I've had ten different jobs in four months."

✳ **T**wo women were out for a Saturday stroll. One had a Doberman Pinscher and the other had a Chihuahua. As they sauntered down the street, the one with the Doberman said to her friend, *"Let's go over to that bar and get something to drink."*

The one with the Chihuahua said, *"We can't go in there. We've got our dogs with us."*

The one with the Doberman said, *"Just follow my lead."*

They walked over to the bar and the one with the Doberman put on a pair of dark glasses and started to walk in.

The bouncer at the door said, *"Sorry, Lady, no pets allowed."*

The woman said, *"You don't understand. This is my seeing-eye dog."*

The bouncer said, *"A Doberman Pinscher?"*

The woman said, *"Yes, they're using them now. They're very good."*

The bouncer said, *"Okay, come on in."*

The lady with the Chihuahua figured, what the heck? It was worth a try. So she put on a pair of dark glasses and started to walk in.

Once again the bouncer said, *"Sorry, Lady, no pets allowed."*

The lady with the Chihuahua said, *"You don't understand. This is my seeing-eye dog."*

The bouncer said, *"They gave you a Chihuahua as a seeing-eye dog?"*

The woman stared at the Bouncer and without blinking an eye said, *"A Chihuahua? They gave me a Chihuahua!!??"*

☯ **A** man and his friend were enjoying opening day of deer hunting season in rural Arkansas near a blacktop highway. A huge buck walked by and the hunter carefully drew his bow and took careful aim.

Before the man could release his arrow, his friend pointed at a funeral procession passing on the road below their stand.

The hunter slowly let off the pressure on his bow, took off his hat, bowed his head and closed his eyes in prayer.

His friend was amazed. *"Wow, that is the most thoughtful and touching thing I have ever seen. You are the kindest man I have ever known."*

The hunter shrugged. *"Yeah, well, we were married for 35 years."*

Bob stood over his tee shot for what seemed an eternity. Finally his partner asked what the holdup was. "My wife is up there watching me from the clubhouse and I want to make a perfect shot." "Good lord!" his buddy exclaimed. "You'll never hit her from here."

A duck goes into a store and says, *"Quack, got any duck food?"*

The gent behind the counter says, *"This is a hardware store. We don't have any duck food."*

The duck goes running out going, *"Quack, quack, quack!"*

The next day the duck goes back to the same store and says, *"Quack, you got any duck food!?"*

The guy says, *"Look, you were here yesterday and I told you we don't carry duck food. So if you come in here again I am going to nail your feet to the floor!"*

The duck goes running out screaming, *"Quack, quack, quack."*

The next day the duck goes back to the same store and says to the guy, *"Got any nails?"*

The guy says, *"No, we just ran out of nails."*

The duck says, *"Good!....got any duck food??!!"*

Billy Bob and Luther were talking one afternoon when Billy Bob tells Luther, *"Ya know, I reckon I'm 'bout ready for a vacation. Only this year I'm gonna do it a little different. The last few years, I took your advice about where to go. Three years ago you said to go to Hawaii. I went to Hawaii and Earlene got pregnant. Then two years ago, you told me to go to the Bahamas, and Earlene got pregnant again. Last year, you suggested Tahiti and darned if Earlene didn't get pregnant again."*

Luther asks Billy Bob, *"So, what you gonna do this year that's different?"*

Billy Bob says, *"This year I'm taking Earlene with me."*

Two guys are wandering about in Home Depot when their carts collide.

One says to the other, *"Sorry, I was looking for my wife."*

"Yeah, so am I, and I'm getting kinda angry that I can't find her."

"Well, let's help each other out. What's your wife look like?"

"Kinda tall, long red hair, long legs, curvaceous body. What's yours look like?"

"Never mind, let's look for yours!"

✈ **W**hile cruising at 36,000 feet, the airplane shuddered, and a passenger looked out the window.

"Oh no!" he screamed, *"One of the engines just blew up!"*

Other passengers left their seats and came running over; suddenly the aircraft was rocked by a second blast as yet another engine exploded on the other side.

The passengers were in a panic now, and even the stewardesses couldn't maintain order. Just then, standing tall and smiling confidently, the pilot strode from the cockpit and assured everyone that there was nothing to worry about. His words and his demeanor made most of the passengers feel better, and they sat down as the pilot calmly walked to the door of the aircraft. There, he grabbed several packages from under the seats and began handing them to the flight attendants. Each crew member attached the package to their backs.

"Say," spoke up an alert passenger, *"aren't those parachutes?"*

The pilot confirmed that they were.

The passenger went on, *"But I thought you said there was nothing to worry about?"*

"There isn't," replied the pilot as a third engine exploded. *"We're going to get help."*

? *"**I** may be blonde, but I'm not dumb. Last year, I replaced all the windows in my house with those expensive dual-pane, energy-efficient kind. This week, I got a call from the contractor complaining that his work had been completed a whole year and I had yet to pay for them.*

Boy, oh boy, did we go around! I proceeded to tell him just what his fast-talking sales guy had told me last year…that in one year the windows would pay for themselves. There was silence on the other end of the line, so I just hung up and he hasn't called back. Guess I won that argument!"

Police are called to an apartment and find a woman holding a bloody 5-iron standing over a lifeless man. The detective asks, *"Ma'am, is that your husband?"*

"Yes," says the woman.

"Did you hit him with that golf club?"

"Yes, yes I did." The woman begins to sob, drops the club and puts her hands on her face.

"How many times did you hit him?"

"I don't know, five, six, maybe seven times…but just put me down for a five!"

🕷 **A** fella is stretched out in his favorite easy chair watching his favorite television program and all of a sudden the door bell rings. He gets up from his chair, obviously very annoyed, opens the door, looks around and finally sees a snail sitting on his door mat. He grabs the snail and angrily throws it as far as he can into his neighbor's garden and goes back to his TV show.

About a year and a half later, he is watching TV again and the door bell rings. He opens the door, looks around and sees the snail again. The snail says, *"So, what was that all about!"*

☯ **T**he divorce court judge says, *"Mr. Clark, I have reviewed this case very carefully, and I've decided to give your wife $775 a week."*

"That's very fair, your Honor," the ex-husband said. *"And every now and then I'll try to send her a few bucks myself!"*

☺ **A**fter the christening of his baby brother in church, Jason sobbed all the way home in the back seat of the car. His father asked him three times what was wrong. Finally, the boy replied, *"That preacher said he wanted us brought up in a Christian home, and I want to stay with you guys."*

⌛ **T**wo old men had been best friends for years, and they both lived to their early 90's, when one of them suddenly fell deathly ill. His friend went to visit him on his deathbed, and they're reminiscing about their long friendship, when the dying man's friend asks, *"Listen, when you die, do me a favor. I want to know if there's baseball in heaven."*

The dying man said, *"We've been friends for years. This I'll do for you."* And then he dies.

A couple days later, his surviving friend is sleeping when he hears his friend's voice. The voice says, *"I've got some good news and some bad news. The good news is that there's baseball in heaven. The bad news is that you're pitching on Wednesday."*

✚ **T**he Doctor called Mrs. Jones to complain saying, *"Mrs. Jones, your check came back."*

"I know, " Mrs. Jones answered, *"so did my arthritis!"*

◪ **A** car hit an elderly Jewish man. As the paramedic works on loading him in the ambulance, he says, *"Are you comfortable?"*

The man says, *"Well, I make a good living."*

?   **A** blonde calls her boyfriend and says, *"Please come over here and help me…I have a killer jigsaw puzzle, and I can't figure out how to get it started."*

Her boyfriend asks, *"What is it supposed to be when it's finished?"*

The blonde says, *"According to the picture on the box, it's a tiger."*

The boyfriend decides to go over and help with the puzzle. She lets him in and shows him where she has the puzzle spread all over the table. He studies the pieces for just a moment, looks at the box they came in, then turns to her and says, *"First of all, no matter what we do, we're not going to be able to assemble these pieces into anything resembling a tiger."*

He holds her hand gently, *"Second, you need to relax…let's have a cup of coffee,"* he sighed. *"Then, we'll put all these Frosted Flakes back in the box."*

⛳   **T**his golfer is whacking his way through some very high weeds and says to his caddy, *"This is a terrible course."*

The caddy says, *"No, it's not. We left the course two or three miles back."*

☯️ **S**he's not the greatest cook, but she is practical. The other day she made me a burger. I couldn't eat it so she used it to clean the sink.

☀️ Great Lines from Rodney Dangerfield

"I could tell that my parents hated me. My bath toys were a toaster and a radio."

"My mother had morning sickness after I was born!"

A girl phoned me and said, 'Come on over, there's nobody home.' I went over. Nobody was home."

"My wife and I were happy for 20 years. Then we met."

"I get no respect from anyone. I bought a cemetery plot. The guy said, 'There goes the neighborhood.'"

"When I was born, I was so ugly that the doctor slapped my mother."

"When my parents got divorced, there was a custody fight over me…and no one showed up."

"When I was 3 years old, my parents got a dog. I was jealous of the dog, so they got rid of me."

✳ **A** guy walks into the local welfare office, marches straight up to the counter and says, *"Hi...you know, I just HATE drawing welfare and I'd really much rather have a job and go to work every day."*

The social worker behind the counter says, *"Your timing is excellent. We just got a job opening from a very wealthy man who wants to hire a chauffeur/bodyguard for his beautiful, 18-year-old daughter. You'll have to drive around in his Mercedes, but he'll supply all of your clothes. Because of the long hours, meals will be provided. You'll be expected to escort her on her overseas holiday trips. You'll have a two-bedroom apartment above the garage. The starting salary is $200,000 a year."*

The guy says, *"You're kidding me!"*

The social worker says, *"Yeah, well, you started it."*

✚ **A** man is recovering from surgery when a nurse asks him how he is feeling.

"I'm okay, but I didn't like the four-letter-word the doctor used in surgery," he answered.

"What did he say?" asked the nurse.

"OOPS!"

? **A** blonde comes home to discover that her apartment is on fire! Her clothes are burning along with her furniture, drapes, everything. She hurries to dial the fire department and screams at them that her apartment is on fire and all of her belongings are burning up. *"You have to come quick!"* she yells.

The fireman on the other end says, *"Okay lady, calm down and just tell us how we get to your apartment."*

She says, *"Well, duh, in the big red truck!"*

☺ **A** mother was preparing pancakes for her sons, Kevin, 5 and Ryan 3. The boys began to argue over who would get the first pancake.

Their mother saw the opportunity for a moral lesson. She said, *"If Jesus were sitting here, He would say, 'Let my brother have the first pancake, I can wait.'"*

Kevin turned to his younger brother and said, *"Ryan, you be Jesus!"*

⚑ **I** can tell this is a golf banquet. Everyone coming to the mike has held it with an interlocking grip.

An engineer died and reported to the pearly gates. An intern angel, filling in for St. Peter, checked his dossier and grimly said, *"Ah, you're an engineer; you're in the wrong place."*

So the engineer was cast down to the gates of hell and was let in. Pretty soon, the engineer became gravely dissatisfied with the level of comfort in hell, and began designing and building improvements. After a while, the underworld had air conditioning, flush toilets, and escalators, and the engineer was becoming a pretty popular guy among the demons.

One day, God called Satan up on the telephone and asked with a sneer, *"So, how's it going down there in hell?"*

Satan laughed and replied, *"Hey, things are going great. We've got air conditioning and flush toilets and escalators, and there's no telling what this engineer is going to come up with next."*

God's face clouded over and he exploded, *"What? You've got an engineer? That's a mistake; he should never have gotten down there; send him up here."*

Satan shook his head, *"No way. I like having an engineer on the staff, and I'm keeping him."*

God was as mad as he had ever been, *"This is not the way things are supposed to work and you know it. Send him back up here or I'll sue."*

Satan laughed uproariously, *"Yeah, right. And just where are YOU going to get a lawyer?"*

🚓 **A** California policeman pulled a car over and told the driver that because he had been wearing his seat belt, he had just won $5,000 dollars in the statewide safety competition.

"What are you going to do with the money?" asked the policeman.

"Well, I guess I'm going to get a driver's license," he answered.

"Oh, don't listen to him," yelled the woman in the passenger seat. *"He's a real jerk when he's drunk."*

This woke up the guy in the back seat, who took one look at the cop and moaned, *"I knew we wouldn't get far in a stolen car."*

At that moment, there was a knock from the trunk and a voice said, in Spanish, *"Are we over the border yet?"*

⏳ **A**n old guy, with Alzheimer's, goes into a cocktail lounge and sees this beautiful lady sitting at the bar. He goes up to her and says, *"Hey, Baby, do I come in here often!"*

❗ *"Do you believe in life after death?"* the boss asked one of his employees.

"Yes, sir, I do." the employee replied.

"Well, then, that makes everything just fine," the boss went on. *"After you left early yesterday to go to your grandmother's funeral, she stopped in to see you."*

⭕ **A** guy goes to a monastery and asks to become a monk.

The abbott says, *"Okay, but you will only be able to say two words every five years."* The guy agrees and disappears into the monastery.

After the first five years he appears in front of the abbott and is asked to say his two words. He says, *"Bed hard."* The abbott nods and makes a note of it.

Five years later, the monk comes back and says *"Food bad."* It is noted, and they don't see him for another five years when he comes back and says, *"I quit."*

With that the abbott looks at him and says, *"Good because all you've done since you've been here is complain!"*

⌛ **A**n elderly couple had dinner at another couple's house, and after eating, the wives left the table and went into the kitchen. The two men were talking, and one said, *"Last night we went out to a new restaurant and it was really great. I would recommend it very highly."*

The other man said, *"What is the name of the restaurant?"*

The first man thought and thought, and finally said, *"What is the name of that flower you give to someone you love? You know...the one that's red and has thorns."*

"Do you mean a rose?"

"Yes, that's the one," replied the man. He then turned towards the kitchen and yelled, *"Rose, what's the name of that restaurant we went to last night?"*

❗ **A** real estate salesman had just closed his first sale, only to discover that the piece of land he had sold was completely under water. *"That customer's going to come back here pretty mad,"* he said to his boss. *"Should I give him his money back?"*

"Money back?" roared the boss. *"What kind of salesman are you? Get out there and sell him a houseboat."*

○　**A**n atheist was taking a walk thru the woods, admiring all that the "accident of evolution" had created.

"What majestic trees! What powerful rivers! What beautiful animals!" he said to himself.

As he walked alongside the river, he heard a rustling in the bushes behind him. As he turned to look, he saw a seven-foot grizzly charge toward him. He ran as fast as he could up the path.

He looked over his shoulder and saw that the bear was gaining on him. He tried to run even faster, so terrified that tears were coming to his eyes.

He look over his shoulder again, the bear was even closer. His heart was pounding as he tried to run faster, but he tripped and fell on the ground. He rolled over and the bear was staring him in the face – raising his paw to kill him.

At that instant he cried out, *"Oh, my God!"*

At that moment, time stopped, the bear froze, the forest was silent, the river stopped moving. A bright light shone upon the man and a voice came out of the heavens saying, *"You deny my existence all these years, teach others I do not exist; even credit my creation to a cosmic accident, and now you expect me to help you out of this predicament? Am I to count you as a believer?"*

The atheist, ever so proud, looked into the light and said, *"It would be rather hypocritical to ask to be a Christian after all these years, but could you make the bear a Christian?"*

"Very well," said the voice of God.

As the light went out, the river flowed, the sounds of the forest continued, the bear put his paw down. The Grizzly then brought both paws together, bowed his head and said, *"Lord, I thank you for this food which I am about to receive!"*

A Polish immigrant goes to the Department of Motor Vehicles to apply for a driver's license and is told he has to take an eye test. The examiner shows him a card with the letters:

C Z J W I X N O S T A C Z

"Can you read this?" the examiner asks.

"Read it?" the Polish guy replies, *"I know the guy."*

He lost only two golf balls last year. He was putting at the time.

Getting away from their high-stress jobs, a couple spends relaxing weekends in their motor home. When they found their peace and quiet disturbed by well-meaning, but unwelcome, visits from other campers, they devised a plan to assure themselves some privacy.

Now, when they set up camp, they place this sign on the door of their RV: "Insurance agents. We have the whole weekend free. Ask how we can help you."

A famous entertainer who has a reputation for stuttering tells the story of his career prior to the entertainment business. His first job was selling bibles and he had a successful technique that he developed as he went door to door.

He knocked on the door and, typically, a lady would answer and gruffly say, *"What do you want?!?"*

"M-m-m-miss, j-j-j-just w-w-w-wondering if you'd l-l-l-like t-t-t-to b-b-b-uy a b-b-b-bible...or would you r-r-r-rather have m-m-me r-r-r-read it t-t-to you?"

Show me a good loser and I'll show you a man who's playing golf with his boss.

☯ **A** man walking along a California beach was deep in prayer. All of a sudden, he said out loud, *"Lord, grant me one wish."* The sky clouded above his head and in a booming voice the Lord said, *"Because you have tried to be faithful to me in all ways, I will grant you one wish."*

The man said, *"Build a bridge to Hawaii so I can drive over anytime I want."*

The Lord said, *"Your request is very materialistic. Think of the enormous challenges for that kind of undertaking. The supports required to reach the bottom of the Pacific and all the concrete and steel it would take! I can do it, but it is hard for me to justify your desire for worldly things. Take a little more time and think of another wish, a wish you think would honor and glorify me."*

The man thought about it for a long time. Finally he said, *"Lord, I wish that I could understand women. I want to know how they feel inside, what they are thinking when they give the silent treatment, why they cry, what they mean when they say 'nothing', and how I can make a woman truly happy."*

The Lord replied, *"You want two lanes or four lanes on that bridge?"*

✚ **I** just left my doctor. I'm okay, but my savings died.

27

☯ **A**n Amish boy and his father were in a mall for the very first time. They were amazed by almost everything they saw, but especially by two shiny, silver walls that could move apart and then slide back together again.

The boy asked, *"What is this Father?"*

The father (never having seen an elevator) responded, *"Son, I have never seen anything like this in my life, I don't know what it is."*

While the boy and his father were watching with amazement, a fat old lady in a wheel chair moved up to the moving walls and pressed a button. The walls opened, and the lady rolled between them into a small room. The walls closed, and the boy and his father watched the small numbers above the walls light up sequentially. They continued to watch until it reached the last number, and then the numbers began to light in the reverse order.

Finally, the walls opened up again and a gorgeous 24-year-old blonde stepped out.

The father, not taking his eyes off the young woman, said quietly to his son, *"Go get your mother."*

? **T**he blonde says to her husband, *"Honey, have you ever noticed in the newspaper that people die in alphabetic order?"*

28

☯ **T**he salesman claimed, *"This encyclopedia will tell you just about everything you need to know."*

The man of the house replied, *"I don't need one. I'm married."*

⧗ **A** senior citizen said to his eighty-year old buddy: *"So I hear you're getting married?"*

"Yep!"

"Do I know her?"

"Nope!"

"This woman, is she good looking?"

"Not really."

"Is she a good cook?"

"Naw, she can't cook too well."

"Does she have lots of money?"

"Nope! Poor as a church mouse."

"Well, then, is she good in bed?"

"I don't know."

"Why in the world do you want to marry her then?"

"Because she can still drive!"

?   Two blondes are in Los Angeles. One blonde asks the other, *"Which is further, London or the moon?"*

The other blonde replies, *"HELLOOOOOOO!!!!! Can you see London from here??????"*

⧗   **A** preacher goes to a nursing home to meet an elderly parishioner. As he is sitting there, he notices this bowl of peanuts beside her bed and takes one. As they talk, he can't help himself and eats one after another.

By the time they are through talking, the bowl is empty. He says, *"Ma'am, I'm sorry, but I seem to have eaten all of your peanuts."*

"That's okay," she says. *"They would have just sat there. Without my teeth, all I can do is suck the chocolate off and put 'em back in the bowl."*

☯   **T**he day after we were married, my wife cooked her first meal. She said, *"Honey, I have a confession to make. I've only learned to cook two things: beef stew and banana pudding."*

I said, *"That's alright dear. I have only one question, which one is this?"*

Employer to applicant: *"In this job we need someone who is responsible."*

Applicant: *"I'm the one you want. On my last job, every time anything went wrong, they said I was responsible."*

Ol' Fred had been a faithful Christian and was in the hospital near death. The family called their pastor to stand with them. As the pastor stood next to the bed, Ol' Fred's condition appeared to deteriorate and he motioned frantically for something to write on. The pastor lovingly handed him a pen and a piece of paper and Ol' Fred used his last bit of energy to scribble a note, then he died. The pastor thought it best not to look at the note at that time, so he placed it in his jacket pocket.

At the funeral, as he was finishing the message, he realized that he was wearing the same jacket that he was wearing when Ol' Fred died. He said, *"You know, Ol' Fred handed me a note just before he died. I haven't looked at it, but knowing Fred, I'm sure there's a word of inspiration there for us all."*

He opened the note and read, *"You're standing on my oxygen tube!!"*

☺ **S**ix-year-old Angie and her four-year-old brother Joel were sitting together in church. Joel giggled, sang, and talked out loud. Finally, his big sister had had enough. *"You're not supposed to talk out loud in church."*

"Why? Who's going to stop me?" Joel asked.

Angie pointed to the back of the church and said, *"See those two men standing by the door? They're the hushers."*

☯ **M**ary Clancy goes up to Father O'Grady after his Sunday morning service and she's in tears.

He says, *"So what's bothering you, Mary, my dear?"*

She says, *"Oh, Father, I've got terrible news. My husband passed away last night."*

The priest says, *"Oh, Mary, that's terrible. Tell me, did he have any last requests?"*

She says, *"That he did, Father."*

The priest says, *"What did he ask, Mary?"*

She says, *"He said, 'Please, Mary, put down the gun!'"*

Bubba's sister is pregnant and is in a bad car accident, which causes her to fall into a deep coma. After nearly six months, she awakens and sees that she is no longer pregnant. Frantically, she asks the doctor about her baby.

The doctor replies, *"Ma'am, you had twins – a girl and a boy. The babies are fine. Your brother came in and named them."*

The woman thinks to herself, *"Oh, no! Not Bubba; he's an idiot."* Expecting the worst, she asks the doctor, *"Well, what's the girl's name?"*

"Denise," the doctor answers.

The new mother says, *"Wow! That's a beautiful name! I guess I was wrong about my brother. I really like the name Denise."*

Then she asks the doctor, *"What's the boy's name?"*

The doctor replies, *"Denephew."*

? **A** highway patrolman pulled alongside a speeding car on the freeway. Glancing at the car, he was astounded to see that the blonde behind the wheel was knitting! Realizing that she was oblivious to his flashing lights and siren, the trooper cranked down his window, turned on his bullhorn and yelled, *"Pull over!"*

"NO!" the blonde yelled back, *"It's a scarf!"*

! **A** salesman walking along the beach found a bottle. When he rubbed it, lo and behold, a genie appeared.

"I will grant you three wishes," announced the genie. *"But since Satan still hates me, for every wish you make, your rival gets the wish as well -- only double."*

The salesman thought about this for a while. *"For my first wish, I would like ten million dollars,"* he announced.

Instantly the genie gave him a Swiss bank account number and assured the man that $10,000,000 had been deposited. *"But your rival has just received $20,000,000,"* the genie said.

"I've always wanted a Ferrari," the salesman said.

Instantly a Ferrari appeared. *"But your rival has just received two Ferraris,"* the genie said. *"And what is your last wish?"*

"Well," said the salesman, *"I've always wanted to donate a kidney for transplant."*

✈ **I**t makes you a bit nervous when you hear the pilot say, *"Now, I guess we'll find out if these seat cushions really do float."*

I had this friend of mine come out to my new course and play and we made a little bet. We get to the first tee. He takes a huge swing and totally misses the ball. He whiffs it. He gets up there again and swings a second time and missed it totally. He does it a third time and says, *"This is the toughest course I have ever played."*

A new hair salon opened up for business right across the street from the old established hair cutters' place.

They put up a big bold sign which read: "WE GIVE SEVEN DOLLAR HAIR CUTS!"

Not to be outdone, the old Master Barber put up his own sign: "WE FIX SEVEN DOLLAR HAIR CUTS."

A fellow was pulled over by the police and one of the policemen says, *"Sir, do you realize that your wife fell out of the car about a mile down the road behind you?"*

The guy says, *"Thank God, I thought I'd gone deaf!"*

✳ **A** guy wakes up one morning to find a bear on his roof. He looks in the yellow pages and, sure enough, finds a bear removal service. When he calls and asks if they can remove the bear, the service guy says he'll be right out.

An hour later, the service guy shows up with a ladder, a baseball bat, a cage, a shotgun and a mean old pit bull. He then gives the man some instructions. *"I'm going to climb up on the roof and poke the bear with the baseball bat until he falls down to the ground, when he does, the pit bull is trained to bite the bear in his private parts and not let go. The bear will then be subdued enough for me to put him in the cage."*

He hands the shotgun to the homeowner. *"What do I do with the shotgun?"* the man asks.

"That's simple," the service guy replies, *"if I fall off the roof before the bear, you shoot the pit bull."*

? **A** blonde was playing Trivial Pursuit one night. It was her turn. She rolled the dice and landed on Science & Nature. Her question was, *"If you are in a vacuum and someone calls your name, can you hear it?"*

She thought for a time and then asked, *"Is the vacuum on or off?"*

?   **A** blonde decides to try horseback riding, even though she has had no lessons or prior experience. She mounts the horse unassisted and the horse immediately springs into motion. It gallops along at a steady and rhythmic pace, but the blonde begins to slip from the saddle. In terror, she grabs for the horse's mane, but cannot seem to get a firm grip. She tries to throw her arms around the horse's neck, but she slides down the side of the horse anyway. The horse gallops along, seemingly ignorant of its slipping rider.

Finally, giving up her frail grip, the blonde attempts to leap away from the horse and throw herself to safety. Unfortunately, her foot becomes entangled in the stirrup, and she is now at the mercy of the horse's pounding hooves as her head is struck against the ground over and over. As her head is battered against the ground, she is mere moments away from unconsciousness when, to her great fortune, Bobby, the Wal-Mart greeter, sees her and unplugs the horse.

⌛   **T**hree old guys are out walking.

The first one says, *"Windy, isn't it?"*

Second one says, *"No, it's Thursday!"*

Third one says, *"Me, too. Let's go for a beer!"*

O **A** Priest, a Pentecostal Preacher and a Rabbi all served as chaplains to the students of the University of Georgia in Athens. They would get together two or three times a week at the Varsity Club for coffee and to talk shop. One day, someone made the comment that preaching to people isn't really all that hard. A real challenge would be to preach to a bear.

One thing led to another and they decided to do an experiment. They would all go out into the woods, find a bear, preach to it, and attempt to convert it.

Seven days later, they're all together to discuss the "experience". Father Flannery, who has his arm in a sling, is on crutches, and has various bandages, goes first. *"Well,"* he says, *"I went into the woods to find a bear. And when I found him I began to read to him from the Catechism. Well, that bear wanted nothing to do with me and began to slap me around. So I quickly grabbed my holy water, sprinkled him and, Holy Mary Mother of God, he became as gentle a lamb. The bishop is coming out next week to give him first communion and confirmation."*

Reverend Billy Bob spoke next. He was in a wheelchair, with an arm and both legs in casts, and an IV drip. In his best fire and brimstone oratory he claimed, *"Well, brothers, you know that we don't sprinkle! I went out and I found a bear. And then I began to read to my bear from God's holy word! But that bear wanted nothing to do with me. So I took hold of him and we began to wrestle. We wrestled down one hill, up another and down another until we came to a creek. So I quick dunked him and baptized his hairy soul. And just like you said, he became as gentle as a lamb. We spent the rest of the day praising Jesus."*

They both looked down at the rabbi, who was lying in a hospital bed. He was in a body cast and traction with IV's and monitors running in and out of him. He was in bad shape.

Rabbi Lipschitz looks up and struggles to speak to the others. *"Looking back on it, circumcision may not have been the best way to start things out."*

A software manager, a hardware manager, and a sales manager are driving to a meeting when a tire blows. They get out of the car and look at the problem.

The software manager says, *"I can't do anything about this - it's a hardware problem."*

The hardware manager says, *"Maybe if we turned the car off and on again, it would fix itself."*

The sales manager says, *"Hey, 75% of it is working. Let's ship it!"*

☯   **A** woman was leaving a Starbucks with her morning coffee when she noticed a most unusual funeral procession approaching the nearby cemetery. A long black hearse was followed by a second long black hearse about 50 feet behind. Behind the second hearse was a solitary woman walking a pit bull on a leash. Behind her were 200 women walking single file.

The woman couldn't stand the curiosity. She respectfully approached the woman walking the dog and said, "I am sorry for your loss and I know now is a bad time to disturb you, but I've never seen a funeral like this. Whose funeral is it?"

The woman replied, *"Well, that first hearse is my husband."*

"What happened to him?"

The woman replied, *"My dog attacked him and killed him."*

She inquired further, *"Well, who is in the second hearse?"*

The woman answered, *"My mother-in-law. She was trying to help my husband when the dog turned on her."*

A poignant and thoughtful moment of silence passes between the two women. *"Could I borrow the dog?"*

"Get in line!"

✳ **T**his is the transcription of the actual radio conversation between the British and the Irish off the coast of Kerry, Ireland in October 1998, released by the Chief of Naval Operations.

IRISH: *"Please divert your course 15 degrees to the South to avoid a collision."*

BRITISH: *"Recommend you divert your course 15 degrees to the North to avoid a collision."*

IRISH: *"Negative. You will have to divert your course 15 degrees to the South to avoid a collision."*

BRITISH: *"This is the Captain of a British Navy Ship. I say again, divert YOUR course."*

IRISH: *"Negative. I say again, you will have to divert YOUR course."*

BRITISH: *"This is the aircraft carrier HMS BRITIANNIA...the second largest ship in the British Atlantic fleet. We are accompanied by three destroyers, three cruisers and numerous support vessels. Demand you change your course 15 degrees north. I say again, that is 15 degrees north or counter measures will be undertaken to ensure the safety of this ship!"*

IRISH: *"We are a lighthouse................Your Call."*

Everybody on earth dies and goes to heaven. God comes and says, *"I want the men to make two lines: one line for the men who dominated their women on earth and the other line for the men who were dominated by their women. Also, I want all the women to go with St. Peter."*

With that said and done, the next time God looked, the women are gone and there are two lines. The line of men that were dominated by their women was 100 miles long, and in the line of men that dominated their women, there was only one man.

God got mad and said, *"You men should be ashamed of yourselves. I created you all in my image and you were all whipped by your mates. Look at the only one of my sons that stood up and made me proud. Learn from him! Tell them, my son, how did you manage to be the only one in this line?"*

And with a proud grin on his face, the man replied, *"My wife told me to stand here."*

Where was the toothbrush invented?

The South. If it was invented anywhere else it would have been called a teethbrush.

🏛 **A** bunch of lawyers were sitting around the office playing poker. *"I win!"* said Johnson, at which point Henderson threw down his cards. *"That's it! I've had it! Johnson is cheating!!!"*

"How can you tell?" Phillips asked.

"Those aren't the cards I dealt him!"

🎖 **P**rivate Jones was assigned to the Army induction center, where he was to advise new recruits about their government benefits, especially their Serviceman's Group Life Insurance (SGLI). It wasn't long before the center's Lieutenant noticed that Private Jones had almost a 100% record for insurance sales, which had never happened before. Rather than ask about this, he stood in the back of the room and listened to Jones's sales pitch.

Jones explained the basics of the SGLI to the new recruits, and then said, *"If you have SGLI and go into battle and are killed, the government has to pay $200,000 to your beneficiaries. If you don't have SGLI, and you go into battle and get killed, the government has to pay only a maximum of $6,000."*

"Now," he concluded, *"which bunch do you think they are going to send into battle first?"*

🕷 **A** man takes a young Rottweiler to the vet and says, *"My dog's cross-eyed, is there anything you can do for him?"*

"Well," says the vet, *"let's have a look at him."* So he picks the dog up and examines his eyes, then checks his teeth. Finally, he says, *"I'm going to have to put him down."*

"What? Because he's cross-eyed?"

"No, because he's really heavy."

☯ **A** woman's husband had been slipping in and out of a coma for several months, yet she had stayed by his bedside every single day.

One day, he motioned for her to come nearer. As she sat by him, he whispered, eyes full of tears, *"You know what? You have been with me through all the bad times. When I got fired, you were there to support me. When my business failed, you were there. When I got shot, you were by my side. When we lost the house, you stayed right here. When my health started failing, you were still by my side. You know what?"*

"What dear?" she gently asked, smiling as her heart began to fill with warmth.

"I think you're bad luck. Get the heck away from me!"

✳   **A** guy is in a crowded movie theater and he is sprawled out over the seats and making funny noises. Finally, a lady close to him gets frustrated and goes to get the manager. She tells the manager that there is a guy down where she is sitting, sprawled out over all the seats and making strange sounds. The manager thanks her and says that he will take care of it.

The manager goes down to where the guy is all spread out and says, *"Sir, please get your legs off of the seats in front of you and your arms off the seats in back of you and just be quiet or I will get the police."* The guy looks up at him and gives him a very strange and painful sound like, *"Aaarugh!"*

The manager says, *"That's it,"* and goes to get a cop to talk to the guy.

The cop goes to where the guy is still moaning and groaning and says, *"Sir, if you don't get those legs off the seats in front of you and your arms off the seats behind you and just straighten up, I am going to throw you out of the theater."*

The guy looks up at the policeman and starts moaning and groaning again, *"Aaarugh!"*

With that the cop says, *"What's your name?"*

He can hardly get it out but he says, *"B-i-l-l."*

The cop says, *"Where are you from?"*

The guy says, *"The b-a-l-c-o-n-y!"*

✳ **C**oach goes into the math professor and says, *"Professor, you're failing my star quarterback because of his math. We'll lose the championship."*

The professor says, *"I don't want that to happen. Bring him in on Saturday. I'll give him an oral quiz and if he does okay on some basic math, I'll go ahead and give him a good grade and we can win the championship."*

The coach brings the kid in and he's sitting there. The coach says, *"C'mon now, prof, make it easy."*

So, the professor says, *"What's 3 times 3?"*

The kid scratches his head and thinks and says, *"Nine."*

The coach jumps up and says, *"Give him another chance! Give him another chance!"*

 When a woman wears leather clothing...

...a man's heart beats quicker, his throat gets dry, he goes weak in the knees and he begins to think irrationally. Ever wonder why?

Because she smells like a new truck.

☀ **D**uring a visit to the mental asylum, a visitor asked the Director what the criterion was which defined whether or not a patient should be institutionalized.

"Well," said the Director, *"first we fill up a bathtub, then we offer a teaspoon, a teacup and a bucket to the patient and ask him or her to empty the bathtub."*

"Oh, I understand," said the visitor. *"A normal person would use the bucket because it's bigger than the spoon or teacup."*

"No," said the Director, *"a normal person would pull the plug. Do you want a room with or without a view?"*

🏛 **A** truck driver was heading down the highway when he saw a priest at the side of the road. Feeling it was his duty, he stopped to give the priest a ride. A short time later, he saw a lawyer with a briefcase on the side of the road and aimed his truck at him. At the last second, he thought of the priest with him and realized he couldn't run over the lawyer. So he swerved, but he heard a thump anyway. Looking back as he drove on, he didn't see anything. He began to apologize for his behavior to the priest. *"I'm sorry, Father. I barely missed that lawyer at the side of the road."*

But the priest said, *"Don't worry, son. I got him with my door."*

○ **T**he new priest is nervous about hearing confessions for the first time, so he asks an older priest to sit in on his sessions.

The new priest hears a couple confessions, then the old priest asks him to step out of the confessional for a few suggestions. The old priest suggests, *"Cross you arms over your chest, and rubyour chin with one hand."*

The new priest tries this.

The old priest suggests, *"Try saying things like, 'I see,' 'yes, go on,' 'I understand' and 'How did you feel about that?'"*

The new priest says those things.

The old priest says, *"Now, don't you think that's a little better than slapping your knee and saying, 'No kidding?!? What happened next?'"*

? **A** police officer stops a blonde for speeding and asks her very nicely if he could see her license.

She replies in a huff, *"I wish you guys would get your act together. Just yesterday you took away my license and then today you expect me to show it to you!"*

A guy comes home, walks in to his wife and says, *"I'm so exhausted."*

His wife says, *"You're exhausted? You played golf all day!"*

He says, *"I know, but let me tell you, Bob and I showed up and it was a full sheet and they put us with two beautiful 20 year old girls...a blonde and a brunette and I am so exhausted."*

She said, *"You mean you played golf with two gorgeous young girls and you're exhausted? Why?"*

He says, *"Honey, have you ever tried to play 18 holes of golf holding your stomach in?"*

The real estate salesman says to his clients, *"This house has both its good points and its bad points. To show you I'm honest, I'm going to tell you about both. The disadvantages are that there is a chemical plant one block south and a slaughterhouse a block north."*

"What are the advantages?" inquired the prospective buyer.

"The advantage is that you can always tell which way the wind is blowing."

? **A** blonde, wanting to earn some money, decided to hire herself out as a handyman-type and started canvassing a wealthy neighborhood. She went to the front door of the first house and asked the owner if he had any jobs for her to do.

"Well, you can paint my porch. How much will you charge?"

The blonde said, *"How about $50?"*

The man agreed and told her that the paint and ladders that she might need were in the garage.

The man's wife, inside the house, heard the conversation and said to her husband, *"Does she realize that the porch goes all the way around the house?"*

The man replied, *"She should. She was standing on it."*

A short time later, the blonde came to the door to collect her money.

"You're finished already?" he asked.

"Yes," the blonde answered, *"and I had paint left over, so I gave it two coats."*

Impressed, the man reached in his pocket for the $50.

"And, by the way," the blonde added, *"that's not a Porch. It's a Ferrari."*

☺ **A** Sunday school teacher asked her class, *"What was Jesus' mother's name?"*

One child answered, *"Mary."*

The teacher then asked, *"Who knows what Jesus' father's name was?"*

A little kid said, *"Verge."*

Confused, the teacher asked, *"Where did you get that?"*

The kid said, *"Well, you know they are always talking about Verge n' Mary."*

☯ **W**hile attending a marriage seminar on communication, Wally and his wife Carolyn listened to the instructor declare, *"It is essential that husbands and wives know the things that are important to each other."*

He addressed the men, *"Can you describe your wife's favorite flower?"*

Wally leaned over, touched Carolyn's arm gently and whispered, *"Pillsbury All-Purpose, isn't it?"* ...and thus began Wally's life of celibacy.

? On a plane bound for New York, the flight attendant approached a blonde sitting in the first class section and requested that she move to economy since she did not have a first class ticket.

The blonde replied, *"I'm blonde, I'm beautiful, I'm going to New York and I'm not moving!"*

Not wanting to argue with a customer, the flight attendant asked the co-pilot to speak with her. He went to talk with the woman asking her to please move out of the first class section.

Again, the blonde replied, *"I'm blonde, I'm beautiful, I'm going to New York and I'm not moving!"*

The co-pilot returned to the cockpit and asked the captain what he should do. The captain said, *"I'm married to a blonde. I know how to handle this."*

He went to the first class section and whispered in the blonde's ear. She immediately jumped up and ran to the economy section mumbling to herself, *"Why didn't anyone just say so?"*

Surprised, the flight attendant and the co-pilot asked what he said to her that finally convinced her to move from her seat. He said, *"I told her that the first class section wasn't going to New York."*

Golfer: *"Caddy, do you think it is a sin to play golf on Sunday?"*

Caddy: *"The way you play, sir, it's a sin any day of the week!"*

☺ A little girl was talking to her teacher about whales.

The teacher said that it was physically impossible for a whale to swallow a human because even though it was a very large mammal, its throat was very small.

The little girl stated that Jonah was swallowed by a whale.

Irritated, the teacher reiterated that a whale could not swallow a human; it was physically impossible.

The little girl said, *"When I get to heaven I will ask Jonah."*

The teacher asked, *"What if Jonah went to hell?"*

The little girl replied, *"Then you ask him."*

○ **A** farmer named Muldoon lived alone in the Irish countryside with a pet dog he doted on. The dog finally died and Muldoon went to the parish priest and asked, *"Father, the dog is dead. Could you be saying a mass for the creature?"*

Father Patrick replied, *"No, we cannot have services for an animal in the church, but there's a new denomination down the road. There's no telling what they believe, but maybe they'll do something for the animal."*

Muldoon said, *"I'll go right now. Do you think $50,000 is enough to donate for the service?"*

Father Patrick asked, *"Why didn't you tell me the dog was Catholic?"*

⧗ **M**orris, an 82 year old man, went to the doctor to get a physical. A few days later, the doctor saw Morris walking down the street with a gorgeous young woman on his arm.

A couple of days later, the doctor spoke to Morris and said, *"You're really doing great, aren't you?"*

Morris replied, *"Just doing what you said, Doc: 'Get a hot mamma and be cheerful.'"*

The doctor said, *"I didn't say that! I said, 'You've got a heart murmur. Be careful.'"*

A salesman dies and is greeted at the Pearly Gates by St. Peter who checks the paper-work and says, *"Hmmm, seems you can go to your choice of either Heaven or Hell. Let me show you what Heaven has to offer."*

St. Peter shows the salesman around. Heaven is a little dull. Lots of people sitting around with the angels listening to music and not doing much of anything except learning to play the harp and singing.

So the salesman decides to visit Hell and see what it has to offer. He's greeted by Satan who gives him the grand tour of a luxurious country club where everyone is playing golf, tennis, beach volleyball, dancing & partying at the bar, and having a grand old time. Satan treats the salesman to a delicious gourmet dinner and promises a great room and VIP tee times if the salesman signs up today.

Of course, the salesman chooses to stay in Hell because it looks like a much more fun way to spend eternity. No sooner does he sign the contract (in blood of course), the country club vanishes and Satan tosses the salesman's soul into the lake of fire.

The salesman cries, *"Hey wait, this isn't what I signed up for! What happened to the country club that was here a minute ago?"*

Satan explains, *"A minute ago you were a prospect. Now you're a client."*

✈ **A** student was heading home for the holidays. When she got to the airline counter, she presented her ticket to New York. As she gave the agent her luggage, she made the remark, *"I'd like you to send my green suitcase to Hawaii, and my red suitcase to London."*

The confused agent said, *"I'm sorry, we can't do that."*

"Really??? I am so relieved to hear you say that because that's exactly what you did to my luggage last year!"

☯ **A** man and his wife, now in their 60's, were celebrating their 40th wedding anniversary. On their special day, a good fairy came to them and said that because they had been such a devoted couple, she would grant each of them a very special wish.

The wife wished for a trip around the world with her husband.

Whoosh! Immediately, she had airline tickets in her hands.

The man wished for a female companion 30 years younger.

Whoosh! Immediately he turned ninety!!!

❋   **T**hree contractors were touring the White House on the same day. One was from Chicago, another from Kentucky, and the third from Florida. At the end of the tour, the guard asked them what they did for a living.

When they each replied that they were contractors the guard said *"Hey, we need one of the rear fences redone. Why don't you guys look at it and give me a bid."* So to the back fence they went.

First up was the Florida contractor. He took out his tape measure and pencil, did some measuring and said, *"Well, I figure the job will run about $900...$400 for materials, $400 for my crew, and $100 profit for me."*

Next was the Kentucky contractor. He also took out his tape measure and pencil, did some quick figuring and said, *"Looks like I can do this job for $700...$300 for materials, $300 for my crew, and $100 profit for me."*

Then the guard asks the Chicago contractor how much. Without so much as moving, the contractor said, *"$2,700."*

The guard, incredulous, looked at him and said, *"You didn't even measure like the other guys! How did you come up with such a high figure?"*

"Easy," said the contractor from Chicago, *"$1,000 for me, $1,000 for you and we hire the guy from Kentucky."*

⧗   **A** couple in their nineties is having problems remembering things. They decide to go to the doctor for a checkup. The doctor tells them that they're physically okay, but they might want to start writing things down to help them remember.

Later that night, while watching TV, the old man gets up from his chair. His wife asks, *"Where are you going?"*

"To the kitchen," he replies.

"Will you get me a bowl of ice cream?"

"Sure."

"Don't you think you should write it down so you can remember it?" she asks.

"No, I can remember it."

"Well, I'd like some strawberries on top, too. You'd better write it down because you know you'll forget it."

He says, *"I can remember that! You want a bowl of ice cream with strawberries."*

"I'd also like whipped cream. I'm certain you'll forget that, so you'd better write it down!" she retorts.

Irritated, he says, *"I don't need to write it down, I can remember it! Leave me alone! Ice cream with strawberries and whipped cream – I got it, for goodness sake!"*

Then he grumbles into the kitchen.

After about 20 minutes the old man returns from the kitchen and hands his wife a plate of bacon and eggs. She stares at the plate for a moment and says, *"Where's my toast?"*

☯   **A** salesman is driving toward home in northern Ontario when he sees an Indian thumbing for a ride on the side of the road. As the trip had been long and quiet, he stops the car and the Indian gets in. After a bit of small talk, the Indian notices a brown bag on the front seat.

"What's in the bag?" asks the Indian.

"It's a bottle of wine. I got it for my wife," says the salesman.

The Indian is silent for a moment and then says, *"Good trade!"*

☺   **A** Sunday school teacher asked her children, as they were on the way to church service, *"And why is it necessary to be quiet in church?"*

One bright little girl replied, *"Because people are sleeping."*

■ **A** man goes into a store and asks the clerk for some "Polish Sausage."

The clerk looked at him and asks, *"Are you Polish?"*

The guy, clearly offended, says, *"Well, yes I am. But let me ask you something. If I asked you for Italian Sausage, would you ask me if I was Italian? Or Hungarian Sausage, would you ask if I was Hungarian? Or, if I asked for German Bratwurst, would you ask me if I was German? Or, if I asked you for a Taco, would you ask me if I was Mexican? Would ya, huh? Would ya?"*

The clerk says, *"Well, no."*

"And if I asked you for some Irish Whiskey, would you ask me if I was Irish? What about Canadian Bacon, would you ask me if I was Canadian?"

"Well, probably not."

With self-indignation, the guy says, *"Well, all right then, why did you ask me if I'm Polish just because I asked for Polish Sausage?"*

The clerk replies, *"Because you're at Home Depot."*

🚩 **H**e doesn't cheat at golf. He just plays for his health. And, of course, a low score just makes him feel much better.

✳ **A** fellow stopped at a rural gas station and, after filling his tank, he bought a soft drink. He stood by his car to drink his cola and he watched a couple of men working along the roadside.

One man would dig a hole two or three feet deep and then move on. The other man came along behind and filled in the hole. While one was digging a new hole, the other was about 25 feet behind filling in the old.

"Hold it, hold it," the fellow said to the men. *"Can you tell me what's going on here with this digging?"*

"Well, we work for the county government," one of the men said.

"But one of you is digging a hole and the other is filling it up. You're not accomplishing anything. Aren't you wasting the county's money?"

"You don't understand, mister," one of the men said, leaning on his shovel and wiping his brow. *"Normally there's three of us, me, Joe and Mike. I dig the hole, Joe sticks in the tree and Mike here puts the dirt back."*

"Yea," piped up Mike. *"Now just because Joe is sick, that doesn't mean we can't work, does it?"*

✳ **A** hip young man goes out and buys the best car available: a Ferrari GTO. It is also the most expensive car in the world and it costs him $500,000. He takes it out for a spin and stops for a red light. An old man on a moped (both looking about 90 years old) pulls up next to him.

The old man looks over at the sleek, shiny car and asks, *"What kind of car ya' got there, sonny?"*

The young man replies, *"A Ferrari GTO, it cost half a million dollars!"*

"That's a lot of money," says the old man. *"Why does it cost so much?"*

"Because this car can do up to 220 miles an hour!" states the young man proudly.

The moped driver asks, *"Mind if I take a look inside?"*

"No problem," replies the owner.

So the old man pokes his head in the window and looks around. Then, sitting back on his moped, the old man says, *"That's a pretty nice car all right!"*

Just then, the light changes so the guy decides to show the old man just what his car can do. He floors it, and within 30 seconds, the speedometer reads 220 mph.

Suddenly, he notices a dot in his rear view

mirror. It seems to be getting closer! He slows down to see what it could be and suddenly, whhooooossshhh! Something whips by him, going much faster!

"What on earth could be going faster than my Ferrari?!" the young man asks himself. Then, ahead of him, he sees a dot coming toward him. Whhooooossshhh!

It goes by again, heading the opposite direction! And it looked like the old man on the moped!

"Couldn't be!" thinks the guy. *"How could a moped outrun a Ferrari?"* But again he sees a dot in his rear view mirror! Whoooosh and KablaMMM! It plows into the back of his car, demolishing the rear end.

The young man jumps out, and it IS the old man!!!

He runs up to the old man and says, *"Oh my gosh!! Is there anything I can do for you?"*

The old man whispers in a raspy breath, *"Unhook...my suspenders...from your side-view mirror..."*

F **Y**ou know you must be creative when playing golf with your boss. You find yourself saying things like, *"You really smacked that one. Did you see how high the water splashed?"*

One Sunday, sitting on the side of the highway waiting to catch speeding drivers, a State Police Officer sees a car puttering along at 22 MPH.

He thinks to himself, *"This driver is just as dangerous as a speeder!"* So he turns on his lights and pulls the driver over.

Approaching the car, he notices that there are five old ladies - two in the front seat and three in the back - wide eyed and white as ghosts. The driver, obviously confused, says to him, *"Officer, I don't understand, I was doing exactly the speed limit! I always go exactly the speed limit. What seems to be the problem?"*

"Ma'am," the officer replies, *"you weren't speeding, but you should know that driving slower than the speed limit can also be a danger to other drivers."*

"Slower than the speed limit? No sir, I was doing the speed limit exactly! Twenty-two miles an hour!" the old woman says a bit proudly.

The State Police officer, trying to contain a chuckle explains to her that "22" was the route number, not the speed limit.

A bit embarrassed, the woman grinned and thanked the officer for pointing out her error.

"But before I let you go, Ma'am, I have to ask, is

everyone in this car OK? These women seem awfully shaken and they haven't muttered a single peep this whole time."

"Oh, they'll be all right in a minute officer. We just got off Route 119."

☯ **A** guy was sitting quietly reading when his wife walked up behind him and whacked him on the head with a newspaper. *"What was that for?"* he asked.

"That was for the piece of paper in your pants pocket with the name Mary Lou written on it," she replied.

"Two weeks ago when I went to the races, Mary Lou was the name of one of the horses I bet on," he explained.

"Oh, honey, I'm sorry," she said. *"I should have known there was a good explanation."*

Three days later he was watching a ball game on TV when she walked up and hit him in the head again, this time with the iron skillet, which knocked him out cold.

When he came to, he asked, *"What was that for?"*

She replied, *"Your horse called."*

God went to the Germans and said, *"I have Commandments for you that will make your lives better."*

And the Germans asked, *"Commandments? What are those?"*

And the Lord said, *"Rules for living."*

"Can you give us an example?"

"Thou shalt not kill."

"Not kill? We're not interested."

So He went to the Italians and said, *"I have Commandments."*

And the Italians wanted an example, and the Lord said, *"Thou shalt not steal."*

"Not steal? We're not interested."

He went to the French and said, *"I have Commandments."*

The French wanted an example, and the Lord said, *"Thou shalt not covet thy neighbor's wife."*

"Not covet my neighbor's wife? We're not interested."

He went to the Jews and said, *"I have Commandments."*

"Commandments?" they said, *"How much are they?"*

"They're free."

"We'll take 10."

? **A** blonde walks by a travel agency and notices a sign in the window, "Cruise Special - $99!"

She goes inside, lays her money on the counter and says, *"I'd like the $99 cruise special, please."*

The agent grabs her, drags her into the back room, ties her to a large inner tube, then drags her out the back door and downhill to the river, where he pushes her in and sends her floating.

A second blonde comes by a few minutes later, sees the sign, goes inside, lays her money on the counter, and asks for the $99 special. She too is tied to an inner tube and sent floating down the river.

Drifting into stronger current, she eventually catches up with the first blonde.

They float side by side for a while before the first blonde asks, *"Do they serve refreshments on this cruise?"*

The second blonde replies, *"They didn't last year."*

An Irishman moves into a tiny village in County Kerry, walks into the pub and promptly orders three beers. The bartender raises his eyebrows, but serves the man three beers, which he drinks quietly at a table, alone. An hour later, the man has finished the three beers and orders three more.

The next evening the man comes in again, orders and drinks three beers at a time, several times. Soon the entire town is whispering about the "Man Who Orders Three Beers."

Finally, a week later, the bartender broaches the subject on behalf of the town. "I don't mean to pry, but folks around here are wondering why you always order three beers?"

"Tis odd, isn't it?" the man replies. *"You see, I have two brothers, and one went to America, and the other to Australia. We promised each other that we would always order an extra two beers whenever we drank as a way of keeping up the family bond."*

The bartender and the whole town were pleased with this answer, and soon the "Man Who Orders Three Beers" became a local celebrity, even to the extent that out-of-towners would come to watch him drink.

Then, one day, the man came in and ordered only two beers. The bartender pours them with a heavy heart. This continues for the rest of the evening; he orders only two beers. The word flies around town. Prayers are offered for the soul of one of the brothers.

The bartender says to the man, *"Folks, around here, me first of all, want to offer condolences to you for the death of your brother. You know, the two beers and all."*

The man ponders this for a moment, then replies, *"You'll be happy to hear that my two brothers are alive and well. It's just that I, meself, have decided to give up drinking for Lent."*

This guy is working with his buddy and says, *"Man, I'm in the doghouse at home."*

His friend says, *"Are you really?"*

He says, *"Yes, I'm in a lot of trouble. My wife made me sleep on the couch and it's such a shame because it was just a slight slip of the tongue yesterday morning."*

His friend asks, *"You mean you got in that much trouble for a slight slip of the tongue?"*

The guy said, *"Yep. That's it. A slight slip of the tongue and she went nuts. We were at the breakfast table and I meant to say, 'Honey, would you pass the butter.' Instead, I said, 'You rotten, no-good witch, you've ruined my entire life.'"*

🚓 **A** police officer pulls over a speeding car. The officer says, *"I clocked you at 80 miles per hours, sir."*

The driver says, *"Gee, officer, I had it on cruise control at 60, perhaps your radar gun needs calibrating."*

Not looking up from her knitting, the wife says, *"Now don't be silly dear, you know that this car doesn't have cruise control."*

As the officer writes out the ticket, the driver looks over at his wife and growls, *"Can't you please keep your mouth shut?"*

The wife smiles demurely and says, *"You should be thankful your radar detector went off when it did."*

As the officer makes out the second ticket for the illegal radar detector, the man glowers at his wife and says through clenched teeth, *"Darn it, woman! Can't you keep your mouth shut?"*

The officer frowns and says, *"And I notice that you're not wearing your seat belt, sir. That's an automatic $75 fine."*

The driver says, *"Yeah, well, you see officer, I had it on but took it off when you pulled me over so that I could get my license out of my back pocket."*

The wife says, *"Now, dear, you know very well that you didn't have your seat belt on. You never wear your seat belt when you're driving."*

And as the police officer is writing out the third ticket the driver turns to his wife and barks, *"WHY DON'T YOU PLEASE SHUT UP!??"*

The officer looks over at the woman and asks, *"Does your husband always talk to you this way Ma'am?"*

"Oh, heavens no, officer. Only when he's been drinking."

Golfer: *"I've played so poorly all day; I think I'm going to go drown myself in that lake."*

Caddy: *"I doubt you could keep your head down that long."*

? An office executive was interviewing a blonde for an assistant position and wanted to find out a little about her personality. *"If you could have a conversation with anyone, alive or dead, who would it be?"*

The blonde thought for a couple of minutes and said, *"I'd have to say the living one!"*

⧖   Jacob, age 92, and Rebecca, age 89, living in Florida, are all excited about their decision to get married. They go for a stroll to discuss the wedding, and on the way they pass a drugstore. Jacob suggests they go in.

Jacob addresses the man behind the counter, *"Are you the owner?"*

The pharmacist answers, *"Yes."*

Jacob says, *"Rebecca and I are about to get married. Do you sell heart medication?"*

The pharmacist answers, *"Of course we do."*

"How about medicine for circulation?"

"All kinds."

"Medicine for rheumatism and scoliosis?"

"Definitely."

"How about Viagra?"

"Of course."

"Medicine for memory problems, arthritis, jaundice?"

"Yes, a large variety. The works."

"What about vitamins, sleeping pills, Geritol, antidotes for Parkinson's disease?"

"Absolutely."

"You sell wheelchairs and walkers?"

"All speeds and sizes. Is there anything else I can help you with?"

"Yes, we'd like to use this store as our Bridal Registry."

☯ **A** doctor examined a woman, took the husband aside and said, *"I don't like the looks of your wife at all."*

"Me either, Doc," said the husband. *"But she's a great cook and really good with the kids."*

▪ **E**mily Sue passed away and Bubba called 911. The 911 operator told Bubba she would send someone out right away. *"Where do you live?"* asked the operator.

Bubba replied, *"At the end of Eucalyptus Drive."*

The operator asked *"Can you spell that for me?"*

There was a long pause and finally Bubba said, *"How 'bout if I drag her over to Oak Street and you pick her up there?"*

? This blonde decides one day that she is sick and tired of all the blonde jokes and how all blondes are perceived as stupid. So, she decides to show her husband that blondes really are smart. While her husband is off at work, she decides that she is going to paint a couple of rooms in the house.

The next day, right after her husband leaves for work, she gets down to the task at hand.

Her husband arrives home at 5:30 and smells the distinctive smell of paint. He walks into the living room and finds his wife lying on the floor in a pool of sweat. He notices that she is wearing a ski jacket and a fur coat at the same time. He goes over and asks her if she is OK. She replies yes.

He then asks what she is doing. She replies that she wanted to prove to him that not all blonde women are dumb and she wanted to do it by painting the house. He then asks her why she has a ski jacket over her fur coat.

She replies that she was reading the directions on the paint can and they said, *"For best results, put on two coats."*

Golfer: *"Do you think I can get on the green with a 5-iron?"*

Caddy: *"Eventually."*

One day my housework-challenged husband decided to wash his sweatshirt. Seconds after he stepped into the laundry room, he shouted to me, *"What setting do I use on the washing machine?"*

"It depends," I replied. *"What does it say on your shirt?"*

He yelled back, *"University of Arizona."* And they say blondes are dumb.

A Denver Broncos fan was enjoying himself at the game in a packed Mile High Stadium, until he noticed an empty seat down in front. He went down and asked the guy next to it if he knew whose seat it was.

The guy said, *"Yes, that's my wife's seat. We have never missed a game since the Craig Morton days, but now my wife is dead."*

The fan offered his sympathy and said it was really too bad that he couldn't find some relative to give the ticket to and enjoy the game together.

"Oh, no." the guy said. *"They're all at the funeral."*

⧗ **S**unday's sermon was "Forgive Your Enemies". Toward the end of the service the Minister asked, *"How many of you have forgiven your enemies?"* Eighty percent of the congregation held up their hands.

He asked them to pray for the strength to forgive. The Minister then repeated his question. All responded this time, except one small elderly lady. *"Mrs. Jones, are you not willing to forgive your enemies?"*

"I don't have any," she replied smiling sweetly.

"Mrs. Jones, that is very unusual. How old are you?"

"Ninety-eight," she answered.

"Oh, Mrs. Jones, please come down to the front and tell us how a person can live ninety-eight years and not have an enemy!"

The little sweetheart of a lady tottered down the aisle, faced the congregation with a beautiful smile and said, *"I outlived all those spiteful people."*

✚ **T**he other day the doctor told me, *"I don't care how you feel. I'll release you from the hospital when I think you're ready to be released and not a dollar sooner."*

✳ **H**ave you ever looked at others your own age and thought, "Surely, I can't look that old?"

I was sitting in the waiting room for my first appointment with a new dentist. I noticed his DDS diploma which bore his full name. Suddenly, I remembered a tall, handsome, dark-haired boy with the same name that had been in my high school class some 40-odd years ago. Could it be the same guy?

Upon seeing him, however, I quickly discarded any such thought. This balding, gray-haired man with the deeply lined face was way too old to have been my classmate. Hmmm...or could it be?

After he examined my teeth, I asked him if he had attended Morgan Park High School. *"Yes, yes I did. I'm a Mustang,"* he gleamed with pride.

"When did you graduate?" I asked.

He answered, *"In 1959. Why do you ask?"*

"You were in my class!" I exclaimed.

He looked at me closely. Then, that ugly, old, wrinkled, jerk asked, *"What did you teach?"*

One dark night outside a small town in Minnesota, a fire started inside the local chemical plant and, in a blink, it exploded into massive flames. The alarm went out to all the fire departments for miles around.

When the volunteer fire fighters appeared on the scene, the chemical company president rushed to the fire chief and said, *"All of our secret formulas are in the vault in the center of the plant and they must be saved! I will give $50,000 to the fire department that brings them out intact."* But the roaring flames held the fire fighters off.

Soon more fire departments had to be called in as the situation became desperate. As the firemen arrived, the president shouted out that the offer was now $100,000 to the fire department who could bring out the company's secret files.

From the distance, a lone siren was heard as another fire truck came into sight. It was the nearby Norwegian rural township volunteer fire company composed mainly of Norwegians over the age of 65.

To everyone's amazement, the little run-down fire engine passed all the newer sleek engines parked outside the plant and drove straight into the middle of the inferno.

Outside, the other firemen watched as the Norwegian old timers jumped off and began to fight the fire with a performance and effort never seen before. Within a short time, the Norse fire fighters had extinguished the fire and saved the secret formulas.

The grateful company president joyfully announced that for such a superhuman feat, he was upping the reward to $200,000.

The local TV news reporters rushed in after capturing the event on film asking *"What are you going to do with all that money?"*

"Vell," said Ole Larsen the 70-year old fire chief, *"da furst thing ve do is fix da brakes on dat truck!"*

⚑ **A** young man and a priest are playing golf together. At a short par-3, the priest asks, *"What are you going to use on this hole, my son?"*

The young man says, *"An 8-iron, Father; how about you?"*

The priest says, *"I'm going to use a soft seven and pray."*

The young man hits his 8-iron and puts the ball on the green.

The priest tops his 7-iron and dribbles the ball out a few yards.

The young man says, *"I don't know about you, Father, but in my church when we pray, we keep our heads down."*

A big city lawyer went duck hunting in rural Texas. He shot and dropped a bird, but it fell into a farmer's field on the other side of a fence.

As the lawyer climbed over the fence, an elderly farmer drove up on his tractor and asked him what he was doing.

The litigator responded, *"I shot a duck and it fell in this field, and now I'm going to retrieve it."*

The old farmer replied, *"This is my property, and you are not coming over here."*

The indignant lawyer said, *"I am one of the best trial attorneys in the United States and, if you don't let me get that duck, I'll sue you and take everything you own."*

The old farmer smiled and said, *"Apparently, you don't know how we settle disputes in Texas. We settle small disagreements like this with the "Three-Kick Rule."*

The lawyer asked, *"What is the Three-Kick Rule?"*

The Farmer replied, *"Well, because the dispute occurs on my land, first I kick you three times and then you kick me three times and so on back and forth until someone gives up."*

The attorney quickly thought about the proposed contest and decided that he could easily take the old codger. He agreed to abide by the local custom.

The old farmer slowly climbed down from the tractor and walked up to the attorney. His first kick planted the toe of his heavy steel-toed work boot into the lawyer's groin and dropped him to his knees. His second kick to the midriff sent the lawyer's last meal gushing from his mouth. The lawyer was on all fours when the farmer's third kick to his rear end sent him face-first into a fresh cow pie. The lawyer summoned every bit of his will and managed to get to his feet.

Wiping his face with the arm of his jacket, he said, *"Okay, now it's my turn."*

The old farmer smiled and said, *"Naw, I give up. You can have the duck."*

❋ The classified ad said, "*Wanted: a very experienced lumberjack.*" A man answered the ad and was asked to describe his experience.

"Well, I've worked in the Sahara Forest."

"You mean the Sahara Desert," said the interviewer.

The man laughed and answered, *"Oh sure, that's what they call it now!"*

❊ **A** couple from Minneapolis decided to go to Florida for a long weekend to thaw out during one particularly icy winter. Because both had jobs, they had difficulty coordinating their travel schedules. It was decided that the husband would fly to Florida on a Thursday, and his wife would follow him the next day. Upon arriving as planned, the husband checked into the hotel. There he decided to open his laptop and send his wife an e-mail back in Minneapolis. However, he accidentally left off one letter in her address, and sent the e-mail without realizing his error.

In Houston, a widow had just returned from her husband's funeral. He was a minister of many years who had been 'called home to glory' following a heart attack. The widow checked her e-mail, expecting messages from relatives and friends. Upon reading the first message, she fainted and fell to the floor. The widow's son rushed into the room, found his mother on the floor, and saw the computer screen which read:

> To: My Loving Wife
> From: Your Departed Husband
> Subject: I've Arrived!
> I've just arrived and have checked in. I see that everything has been prepared for your arrival tomorrow. Looking forward to seeing you then! Hope your journey is as uneventful as mine was.

(P.S. Sure is hot down here!)

✳ **A** dinner speaker was in such a hurry to get to his engagement that when he arrived and sat down at the head table, he suddenly realized that he had forgotten his false teeth.

Turning to the man next to him he said, *"I can't believe what I've done. I forgot my teeth."*

The man said, *"No problem."* With that he reached into his pocket and pulled out a pair of false teeth. *"Try these,"* he said.

The speaker tried them. *"Too loose,"* he said.

The man then said, *"I have another pair...try these."*

The speaker tried them and responded, *"Too tight."*

The man was not taken back at all. He then said, *"I have one more pair of false teeth...try them."*

The speaker said, *"They fit perfectly."*

With that he ate his meal and gave his address. After the dinner meeting was over, the speaker went over to thank the man who had helped him. *"I want to thank you for coming to my aid. Where is your office? I've been looking for a good dentist."*

The man replied, *"I'm not a dentist. I'm the local undertaker."*

☯ **A** husband was in big trouble when he forgot his wedding anniversary. His wife told him, *"Tomorrow there better be something in the driveway for me that goes zero to 200 in 2 seconds flat."*

The next morning the wife found a small package in the driveway. She opened it and found a brand new bathroom scale.

Funeral arrangements for the husband have been set for Saturday.

◼ **A** Polish guy goes into the Doctor complaining of pain and the doctor asks what's wrong.

He says, *"Doc, whenever I touch my head with my finger like this it hurts; and whenever I touch my arm with my finger like this it hurts; and whenever I touch my ribs like this it hurts; even when I touch my stomach, my leg, and my face, it hurts."*

The Doctor says, *"You're Polish, aren't you?"*

The guy says *"Yes, how could you know that?"*

The doctor says, *"Well, because your finger is broken!"*

🕷 **D**uring the Super Bowl, there was another football game of note between the big animals and the little animals. The big animals were crushing little animals and at half-time, the coach made a passionate speech to rally the little animals.

At the start of the second half the big animals had the ball. The first play, the elephant got stopped for no gain. The second play, the rhino was stopped for no gain. On third down, the hippo was thrown for a 5 yard loss.

The defense huddled around the coach and he asked excitedly, *"Who stopped the elephant?"*

"I did," said the centipede.

"Who stopped the rhino?"

"Uh, that was me too," said the centipede.

"And how about the hippo? Who hit him for a 5 yard loss?"

"Well, that was me as well," said the centipede.

"So where were you during the first half?" demanded the coach.

"Well," said the centipede, *"I was having my ankles taped."*

○ Four Jewish gentlemen meet every Saturday for golf. They always shoot around 100. Once in awhile they'll break 100. This one week, they meet and three of the fellas shoot in the low 80s and Abe shoots a 102. So they come in and Abe says, *"What's with your game? We hardly ever break 100."*

And they all say, *"We've been going to the temple every morning."*

Abe says, *"That's how you score in the 80s? I'm doing it, too."*

So, Abe goes every day to the temple. When they meet the next time, the other three shoot in the low 80s again. Abe shoots 102. He says, *"What's going on? I did what you told me. I went to the temple every day and I can't break 100."*

They said, *"Abe, what temple did you go to?"*

He said, *"Temple Emmanuel."*

His friends say, *"No, no, no, no. That one's for tennis!"*

✳ Two cannibals are eating a clown in the jungle and one turns to the other and says, *"Does this meat taste funny to you!?"*

☯ **J**ohn and Mary's marriage is a 50/50 deal. Half the time she's right and half the time, he's wrong.

? **A** guy took his blonde girlfriend to her first football game. They had great seats right behind their team's bench. After the game, he asked her how she liked the experience.

"Oh, I really liked it," she replied, *"especially the tight pants and all the big muscles, but I just couldn't understand why they were killing each other over 25 cents."*

Dumbfounded, her date asked, *"What do you mean 25 cents?"*

"Well, they flipped a coin, one team got it and then for the rest of the game, all they kept screaming was: 'Get the quarterback! Get the quarterback!' I'm like... Helloooo? It's only 25 cents!!!!"

🚓 **A** tourist asks a man in uniform, *"Are you a policeman?"*

"No, I am an undercover detective."

"So why are you in uniform?"

"Today is my day off."

⛳ **T**he course I play is getting tougher. They've increased the speed of the windmill and narrowed the clown's mouth.

🏆 **T**he sales manager addressing an under performing sales force at the start of a new month: *"We are going to have a sales contest this month. The winners will get to enter next month's contest."*

☯ **A**s the man of the house, I was tired of being bossed around by my wife; so I went to a psychiatrist. The psychiatrist said I needed to build my self-esteem, and so he gave me a book on assertiveness, which I read on the way home.

I finished the book by the time I reached my house. I stormed into the house and walked up to my wife.

Pointing a finger in her face, I said, *"From now on, I want you to know that I'm the man of this house and my word is law! I want you to prepare me a gourmet meal tonight and when I'm finished eating the meal, I expect a sumptuous dessert. Then, after dinner, you're going to draw me my bath so I can relax. And, when I'm finished with my bath, guess who's going to dress me and comb my hair?"*

She said, *"The funeral director."*

✳ **T**he local bar was so sure that its bartender was the strongest man around that they offered a standing $1,000 bet: The bartender would squeeze a lemon until all the juice ran into a glass, and hand the lemon to a patron. Anyone who could squeeze out one more drop of juice would win the money. Many people had tried over time but nobody could do it.

One day this scrawny little man came into the bar, wearing thick glasses and a polyester suit, and said in a tiny squeaky voice, *"I'd like to try the bet."*

After the laughter died down, the bartender said OK, grabbed a lemon, and squeezed away. Then he handed the wrinkled remains of the rind to the little man. The crowd's laughter turned to total silence as the man clenched his fist around the lemon and six drops fell into the glass.

As the crowd cheered, the bartender paid the $1000, and asked the little man, *"What do you do for a living? Are you a lumberjack, a weightlifter, or what?"*

The man replied, *"I work for the IRS."*

✳ **W**hat's the definition of an optimist?

A folk musician with a mortgage.

⌛ You Know You're Getting Older When...

1. Everything hurts and what doesn't hurt doesn't work.

2. The gleam in your eyes is from the sun hitting your bifocals.

3. You feel like the morning after and you haven't been anywhere.

4. Your little black book contains only names that end in M.D.

5. Your children begin to look middle aged.

6. You finally reach the top of the ladder and find it leaning against the wrong wall.

7. Your mind makes contracts your body can't meet.

8. You look forward to a dull evening.

9. Your favorite part of the newspaper is "20 Years Ago Today."

10. You turn out the lights for economic rather than romantic reasons.

11. You sit in a rocking chair and can't get it going.

12. Your knees buckle, and your belt won't.

13. Your back goes out more than you do.

14. Your Pacemaker makes the garage door go up when you see a pretty girl.

15. The little old gray haired lady you helped across the street is your wife.

16. You sink your teeth into a steak, and they stay there.

17. You have too much room in the house and not enough in the medicine cabinet.

18. You know all the answers, but nobody asks you the questions.

19. You're asleep, but others worry that you're dead.

20. You quit trying to hold your stomach in, no matter who walks into the room.

21. Your best friend is dating someone half their age...and isn't breaking any laws.

22. You sing along with the elevator music.

23. You enjoy hearing about other people's operations.

24. People call at 9 p.m. and ask, "Did I wake you?"

25. Your ears are hairier than your head.

26. You got cable for the weather channel.

27. You have a party and the neighbors don't even realize it.

☺   **T**wo little kids are in a hospital, lying on stretchers next to each other, outside the operating room.

The first kid leans over and asks, *"What are you in here for?"*

The second kid says, *"I'm in here to get my tonsils out and I'm a little scared."*

The first kid says, *"You've got nothing to worry about. I had that done when I was four. They put you to sleep, and when you wake up they give you lots of Jell-O and ice cream. It's a breeze."*

The second kid then asks, *"What are you here for?"*

The first kid says, *"A circumcision."*

The second kid replies, *"Whoa, good luck buddy. I had that done when I was born and, man, I couldn't walk for a year!"*

☯   *C*ash, check or charge?" I asked after folding items the woman wished to purchase. As she fumbled for her wallet I notice a remote control for a television set in her purse. *"Do you always carry your TV remote?"* I asked. *"No,"* she replied. *"But my husband refused to come shopping with me, so I figured this was the most evil thing I could do to him."*

One afternoon, a wealthy lawyer was riding in the back of his limousine when he saw two men eating grass by the road side. He ordered his driver to stop and he got out to investigate.

"Why are you eating grass?," he asked one man.

"We don't have any money for food," the poor man replied.

"Oh, come along with me then."

"But sir, I have a wife with two children!"

"Bring them along! And you, come with us too!" he said to the other man.

"But sir, I have a wife with six children!" the second man answered.

"Bring them as well!"

They all climbed into the car, which was no easy task, even for a car as large as the limo.

Once underway, one of the poor fellows says, *"Sir, you are too kind. Thank you for taking all of us with you."*

The lawyer replied, *"No problem, the grass at my home is about two feet tall."*

✝ **A** woman, calling a local hospital, said, *"Hello, I'd like to talk with the person who gives the information regarding your patients. I'd like to find out if a patient is getting better, or doing as expected, or is getting worse?"*

The voice on the other end of the line said, *"What is the patient's name and room number?"*

"Sarah Finkel in room 302."

"I will connect you with the nursing station."

"3-A Nursing Station. How can I help you?"

"I would like to know the condition of Sarah Finkel in Room 302."

"Just a moment. Let me look at her records. Oh, yes. Mrs. Finkel is doing very well. In fact, she's had two full meals. Her blood pressure is fine. Her blood work just came back as normal. She's going to be taken off the heart monitor in a couple of hours and if she continues this improvement, Dr. Cohen is going to send her home Tuesday at twelve o'clock."

The woman said, *"Thank God! That's wonderful! Oh! That's fantastic….that's wonderful news!"*

The nurse said, *"From your enthusiasm, I take it you must be a close family member or a very close friend?"*

"Not exactly, I'm Sarah Finkel in 302! Nobody here tells me anything!!"

How many salespeople does it take to replace a light bulb?

Two. One to say that it has a life-time guarantee and the other one to say that it has a money-back guarantee.

A guy says to his friend, *"What a game I'm playing today. Look at this new ball."*

He hands it to the friend. The friend says, *"What's so special about it?"*

The guy says, *"I can't lose this ball."*

The friend says, *"I know your game. You could lose any ball."*

The guy says, *"Not this ball. This is high technology. There's a sensor built inside. If it goes into the rough, it knows I can't see it and it'll beep so I can find it. And, of course, if it goes where I could see it, it has a flasher to help me find it. If it goes in the water, it has this little dot, do you see it? That opens when it hits the water. A sail comes out and the wind will blow it over and I keep it. I never lose it."*

The friend says, *"I love that ball. I've gotta get one. Where do I buy one?"*

The guy says, *"I don't know. I found it."*

A man goes to see the Rabbi. *"Rabbi, something terrible is happening and I have to talk to you about it."*

The Rabbi asked, *"What's wrong?"*

The man replied, *"My wife is poisoning me."*

The Rabbi, very surprised by this, asks, *"How can that be?"*

The man then pleads, *"I'm telling you, I'm certain she's poisoning me. What should I do?"*

The Rabbi then says, *"Tell you what...let me talk to her, and I'll see what I can find out and I'll let you know."*

A week later the Rabbi calls the man and says, *"Well, I spoke to your wife. I spoke to her on the phone for four hours. You want my advice?"*

The man said, *"Yes, Rabbi, of course!"*

To which the Rabbi replied, *"Take the poison!"*

To the caddy, *"Why do you keep looking at your watch?"*

The caddy replies, *"It's not my watch, sir. It's my compass."*

✳ **T**hree men took a small plane to the wilderness in northern Canada to hunt moose over the weekend. The last thing the pilot said was, *"Remember, this is a very small plane and you will only be able to bring ONE moose back."*

But of course, they killed one each and returned to the plane with three moose.

The pilot said, *"I told you to bring one moose only."*

"That's what you told us last year," the hunters replied, *"but for an additional $100 you allowed us to bring three moose. Here, take the $100 now."*

The pilot agrees, and lets them bring all three dead moose onboard.

Just after takeoff, the plane stalled and crashed. In the wreckage, one of the men woke up, looked around and said, *"Where the heck are we?"*

"Oh, just about a hundred yards east of the place where we crashed last year."

❢ **L**ife insurance agent to would-be client: *"Don't let me frighten you into a hasty decision. Sleep on it tonight. If you wake in the morning, give me a call then and let me know."*

Sadly, Dave was born without ears, and though he proved to be successful in business, his problem annoyed him greatly. One day, he needed to hire a new manager for his company, so he set up three interviews.

The first guy was great. He knew everything he needed to know and was very interesting. But at the end of the interview, Dave asked him, *"Do you notice anything different about me?"*

"Why, yes, I couldn't help but notice that you have no ears," came the reply. Dave did not appreciate his candor and threw him out of the office.

The second interview was with a woman, and she was even better than the first guy. But he asked the same question, *"Do you notice anything different about me?"*

"Well," she said stammering, *"You have no ears."* Dave again got upset and chucked her out in a rage.

The third and final interviewee was the best of the bunch. He was a young man who recently earned his MBA. He was smart, handsome and seemed to be a better businessman than the first two put together. Dave was anxious but went ahead and asked the young man the same question, *"Do you notice anything different about me?"*

Much to his surprise, the young man answered,

"Yes, you wear contact lenses, don't you?"

Dave was shocked and realized this was an incredibly observant person.

"How in the world did you know that?" he asked.

The young man fell of his chair laughing hysterically and replied, *"Well, it's pretty hard to wear glasses when you have NO EARS!"*

? **A** blonde was terribly overweight, so her doctor put her on a diet.

"I want you to eat regularly for 2 days, then skip a day, and repeat this procedure for 2 weeks. The next time I see you, you'll have lost 5 pounds."

When the blonde returned, she shocked the doctor by losing nearly 20 pounds.

"Why, that's amazing!" the doctor said, *"Did you follow my instructions?"*

The blonde nodded, *"I'll tell you though, I thought I was going to drop dead that 3rd day!"*

"From hunger, you mean?" asked the doctor.

"No, from skipping!"

✚ Things You Don't Want to Hear During Surgery

"Better save that. We'll need it for the autopsy."

"No! No! Come back with that! Bad Dog!"

"Wait a minute, if this is his spleen, what's that?"

"Hand me that…uh…that uh…thingie."

"Oops! Hey, has anyone ever survived 500ml of this stuff?"

"There go the lights again."

"Ya know, there's big money in kidneys and this guy has two of 'em."

"Everybody stand back! I lost my contact lens."

"What's this doing here?"

"Sterile, shmerile. The floor's clean, right?"

"What do you mean he wasn't in for a sex change?"

"Nurse, did this patient sign the organ donor card?"

"Don't worry. I think it's sharp enough."

"Uh-oh! Page 47 of the manual is missing."

"Well, folks, this will be a new experience for all of us."

"This patient has already had some kids, am I correct?"

A man calls home to his wife and says, *"Honey, I have been asked to go fishing at a big lake up in Canada with my boss and several of his friends. We'll be gone for a week. This is a good opportunity for me to get that promotion I've been wanting. So, would you please pack me enough clothes for a week and set out my rod and tackle box? We're leaving from the office and I will swing by the house to pick up my things. Oh! Please pack my new blue silk pajamas."*

The wife thinks this sounds a little fishy but, being a good wife, she does exactly what her husband asked.

The following weekend he comes home a little tired but otherwise looking good. The wife welcomes him home and asks if he caught many fish. He says, *"Yes! Lot's of Walleye, some Bluegill and a few Pike. But why didn't you pack my new blue silk pajamas like I asked you to do?"*

The wife replies, *"I did. They were in your tackle box!"*

Golfer: *"That can't be my ball, caddy. It looks far too old."*

Caddy: *"It's a long time since we started, sir."*

A woman comes home and says to her husband, *"Honey, we have trouble with the car."*

He says, *"What's it doing this time?"*

She says, *"I think it is water in the carburetor."*

He says, *"You don't know anything about cars. You wouldn't know water in the carburetor from water on your brain!"*

She says, *"Well, I think it's water in the carburetor."*

He says, *"Okay, where is the car?"*

She says, *"It's in the pool!"*

What if Saddam Hussein survived all the bombings, but lost a leg?

How stressed out do you think his doubles would be?

Golfer: *"Well, I have never played this badly before!"*

Caddy: *"I didn't realize that you had ever played before, sir."*

◯ **A** lady went to her priest one day and told him, *"Father, I have a problem. I have two female parrots, but they only know how to say one thing."*

"What do they say?" the priest inquired.

It's so embarrassing, Father. *"They say, 'Hi, we're in sales. Do you want to have some fun?'"*

"That's obscene!" the priest exclaimed. Then he thought for a moment. *"You know,"* he said, *"I may have a solution to your problem. I have two male talking parrots whom I have taught to pray and read the Bible. Bring your two parrots over to my house, and we'll put them in the cage with Francis and Job. My parrots can teach your parrots to praise and worship, and your parrots are sure to stop saying 'that' phrase in no time."*

"Thank you," the woman responded, *"this may very well be the solution."*

The next day she brought her female parrots to the priest's house. As he ushered her in, she saw that his two male parrots were inside their cage, holding rosary beads and praying. Impressed, she walked over and placed her parrots in with them. After a few minutes, the female parrots cried out in unison: *"Hi, we're in sales. Do you want to have some fun?"*

There was stunned silence. Finally, one male parrot looked over at the other male parrot and exclaimed, *"Put the beads away, Francis. Our prayers have been answered!"*

♀ **A** shepherd is looking after his sheep on the side of a lonely hill, across which winds a narrow road. Suddenly, a brand new Porsche screeches to a halt. The driver, a young man in an Armani suit, gets out and asks the shepherd. *"If I can tell you how many sheep you have, will you give me one of them?"*

The shepherd looks at the young man and his large flock of sheep and replies, *"Okay."*

The young man parks his car, connects his laptop to his mobile fax, enters the NASA website, scans the ground using his GPS, opens a database and Excel files filled with pivot tables, then prints out a 150-page report on his hi-tech mini printer. He then turns to the shepherd and says, *"You have exactly 1,586 sheep."*

The shepherd answers, *"That's correct. You can have your choice of sheep."*

The young man picks up an animal and puts it in the back of his Porsche. The shepherd looks at him and asks. *"If I guess your profession, will you return my animal to me?"*

The young man answers, *"Yes, why not?"*

The shepherd says, *"You're a management consultant."*

"How did you know?" gasps the young man.

"Very simple," answers the shepherd. *"First, you came here without being asked. Second, you*

charged me a fee to tell me something that I already knew. Third, you don't understand anything about my business. Now, may I have my dog back?"

✈ **Y**ou know, I fly a lot and certain things make me nervous. The other day I heard the pilot say, *"Hey, I ain't gonna try and land this big ol' thing in the dark."*

❓ **A** blonde calls Delta Airlines and asks, *"Can you tell me how long it'll take to fly from San Francisco to New York City?"*

The agent replies, *"Just a minute…"*

"Thank you," the blonde says and hangs up!

✚ **H**ow many psychologists does it take to change a light bulb?

None. The light bulb will change itself when it's ready.

Just one, but the light bulb really has to want to change.

   A new book on golf just came out. It gives the reader valuable playing tips and insider information from the author's 18 years of experience. The following chapter listing gives you an overview of the book. Don't wait until they're all gone!!

Chapter 1 - How to Properly Line Up Your
    Fourth Putt

Chapter 2 - How to Hit a Nike from the Rough
    When You Hit a Titleist from the Tee

Chapter 3 - How to Avoid the Water When You
    Lie 8 in a Bunker

Chapter 4 - How to Get More Distance Off the
    Shank

Chapter 5 - When to Give the Ranger the Finger

Chapter 6 - Using Your Shadow on the Greens to
    Maximize Earnings

Chapter 7 - When to Implement Handicap
    Management

Chapter 8 - Proper Excuses for Drinking Beer
    Before 9 AM

Chapter 9 - How to Rationalize a 6 Hour Round

Chapter 10 - How to Find That Ball That
    Everyone Else Saw Go in the Water

Chapter 11 - Why Your Spouse Doesn't Care
    That You Birdied the 5th

◯ **D**o you know how you get 49 out of 50 nuns to all swear at the same time?

Just have the 50th one say, *"Bingo!"*

✚ **M**y doctor says, *"I'm well aware that the cost of medical care is outrageous but so is the price of yachts."*

107

☯   **A** woman was out golfing one day when she hit a ball into the woods. She went into the woods to look for it and found a frog in a trap. The frog said to her, *"If you release me from this trap, I will grant you three wishes."*

The woman freed the frog, and the frog said, *"Thank you, but I failed to mention the condition to your wishes. Whatever you wish for, your husband will get times ten!"*

The woman said, *"That's okay."*

For her first wish, she wanted to be the most beautiful woman in the world.

The frog warned her, *"You do realize that this wish will also make your husband the most handsome man in the world, an Adonis whom women will flock to."*

The woman replied, *"That's okay, because I will be the most beautiful woman and he will have eyes only for me."* So, KAZAM — she's the most beautiful woman in the world.

For her second wish, she wanted to be the richest woman in the world.

The frog said, *"That will make your husband the richest man in the world. And he will be ten times richer than you."*

The woman said, *"That's okay, because what's*

mine is his and what's his is mine."

So, KAZAM — she's the richest woman in the world.

The frog then inquired about her third wish, and she answered, *"I'd like a mild heart attack."*

Moral of the story: Women are clever. Don't mess with them.

Attention female readers: This is the end of the joke for you. Stop here and continue feeling good.

Attention male readers: Please read on.

The man had a heart attack ten times milder than his wife.

Moral of the story: Women think they're really smart. Let them continue to think that way and just enjoy the show.

Golfer: *"Caddy, do you think my game is improving?"*

Caddy: *"Oh, yes, sir! You miss the ball much closer than you used to."*

✳ New Proverbs

Before you criticize someone, walk a mile in his shoes. That way, if he gets angry, he'll be a mile away – and barefoot.

Artificial intelligence is no match for natural stupidity.

A clear conscience is usually the sign of a bad memory.

My idea of housework is to sweep the room with a glance.

It is easier to get forgiveness than permission.

If you look like your passport picture, you probably need the trip.

Always yield to temptation, because it may not pass your way again.

Bills travel through the mail at twice the speed of checks.

Eat well, stay fit, die anyway.

Men are from earth. Women are from earth. Deal with it!

Age is a very high price to pay for maturity.

Going to church doesn't make you a Christian any more than going to a garage makes you a mechanic.

A conscience is what hurts when all your other parts feel so good.

✳ **New Bumper Stickers**

If You Can't Feed Em, Don't Breed Em!

If You Can Read This, I've Lost My Trailer.

Cleverly Disguised As A Responsible Adult.

If We Quit Voting, Will They All Go Away?

Honk If Anything Falls Off.

Cover Me, I'm Changing Lanes.

He Who Hesitates Not Only Is Lost, But is Miles From The Next Exit.

(Seen Upside Down On A Jeep) If You Can Read This, Please Flip Me Back Over.

Guys: No Shirt, No Service
Gals: No Shirt, No Charge

? **A** blonde said, *"I was worried that my mechanic might try to rip me off. I was relieved when he told me all I needed was turn signal fluid."*

☯ **T**he other day, she threw him out of the house. Unfortunately, they live in an RV and were doing 70 miles an hour at the time.

❄ **A** man in Phoenix calls his son in New York and says, *"I hate to ruin your day, but I have to tell you that your mother and I are divorcing. Forty-five years of misery is enough."*

"Pop, what are you talking about?" the son screams.

"We can't stand the sight of each other any longer," the old man says. *"We're sick of each other, and I am sick of talking about this. So you call your sister in Chicago and tell her,"* and hangs up.

Frantic, the son calls his sister, who explodes on the phone. *"Like heck they're getting divorced,"* she shouts. *"I'll take care of this."*

She calls Phoenix immediately and screams at the old man. *"You are NOT getting divorced. Don't do a thing until I get there. I'm calling my brother back, and we'll both be there tomorrow. Until then, don't do a thing, DO YOU HEAR ME?"* and hangs up.

The old man hangs up his phone and turns to his wife. *"Okay,"* he says, *"they're both coming for Christmas and paying their own way."*

☯ **S**omeone stole all my credit cards, but I won't be reporting it. The thief spends less than my wife did.

A Mexican bandit made a specialty of crossing the Rio Grande from time to time and robbing banks in Texas. Finally, a reward was offered for his capture, and an enterprising Texas ranger decided to track him down.

After a lengthy search, he traced the bandit to his favorite cantina, snuck up behind him, put his trusty six-shooter to the bandit's head, and said, *"You're under arrest. Tell me where you hid the loot or I'll blow your brains out."*

But the bandit didn't speak English, and the Ranger didn't speak Spanish. Fortunately, a bilingual lawyer was in the saloon and translated the Ranger's message. The terrified bandit blurted out, in Spanish, that the loot was buried under the oak tree in back of the cantina.

"What did he say?" asked the Ranger.

The lawyer answered, *"He said 'Get lost, you turkey. You wouldn't dare shoot me.'"*

A woman went to the Post Office to buy stamps for her Christmas Cards. *"What denomination?"* asked the clerk.

"Oh, good heavens! Have we come to this?" said the woman. *"Well, give me 30 Catholic, 10 Baptist ones, 20 Lutheran, and 40 Presbyterian."*

◯ **W**hile the Pope was visiting the USA, he told the driver of his limo that he had the urge to drive. The driver was a good Catholic man, and would not ever dream of questioning the Pope's authority. So, the Pope sat at the wheel, while his driver got in the back.

They were traveling down the road doing between 70 and 80 mph when a policeman happened to see them. As he pulled them over, he called in to headquarters reporting a speeding limo, with a VIP inside it

The chief asked, *"Who is in the limo, the mayor?"*

The policeman told him, *"No, someone more important than the mayor."*

Then the chief asked, *"Is it the governor?"*

The policeman answered, *"No, someone more important than the governor."*

The chief finally asked, *"Is it the President?"*

The policeman answered, *"No, someone even more important than the President."* This made the chief very angry and he bellowed, *"Now who is more important than the President?!"*

The policeman calmly whispered, *"I'll put it to you this way chief. I don't know who this guy is, but he has the Pope as his chauffeur."*

✳ **A** guy rushes into a bar, orders four expensive 30-year-old single malts and has the bartender line them up in front of him. Then without pausing, he quickly downs each one. *"Whew,"* the bartender remarked, *"you seem to be in a hurry."*

"You would be too if you had what I have."

"What do you have?" the bartender sympathetically asked.

"Fifty cents."

❗ **T**wo shoe salespeople were sent to Africa to open up new markets.

Three days after arriving, one salesperson called the office and said, *"I'm returning on the next flight. Can't sell shoes here. Everybody goes barefoot."*

At the same time the other salesperson sent an e-mail to the factory, saying, *"The prospects are unlimited. Nobody wears shoes here!"*

⛳ **G**olfer (screaming): *"You've got to be the worst caddy in the world."*

Caddy: *"I doubt it. That would be too much of a coincidence!"*

❖ A salesman was demonstrating unbreakable combs in a department store. He was impressing the people who stopped by to look by putting the comb through all sorts of torture and stress.

Finally, to impress even the skeptics in the crowd, he bent the comb completely in half, and it snapped with a loud crack. Without missing a beat, he bravely held up both halves of the 'unbreakable' comb for everyone to see and said, *"And this, ladies and gentlemen, is what an unbreakable comb looks like on the inside."*

⌛ Two seniors are standing in front of the Hotel Duluth when they see a penguin walking by. Pat grabs it and asks Mike, *"What should I do with him?"*

Mike says, *"Why don't you take him to the zoo?"*

The next day in front of the same hotel, Mike sees Pat walking with the penguin on a leash. *"I thought I told you to take him to the zoo,"* says Mike.

"I did," says Pat, *"and we had such a good time that tonight I think I'll take him to the hockey game!"*

✳ **A** film crew was on location deep in the desert. One day an old Indian went up to the director and said, *"Tomorrow rain."* The next day it rained.

A week later, the Indian went up to the director and said, *"Tomorrow storm."* The next day there was a hailstorm.

"This Indian is incredible," said the director. He told his secretary to hire the Indian to predict the weather. However, after several successful predictions, the old Indian didn't show up for nearly two weeks.

Finally the director sent for him. *"I have to shoot a big scene tomorrow,"* said the director, *"and I'm depending on you. What will the weather be like?"*

The Indian shrugged his shoulders. *"Don't know,"* he said. *"Radio broken."*

🚓 **A** policeman pulls a man over for speeding and asks him to get out of the car. After looking the man over he says, *"Sir, I couldn't help but notice your eyes are bloodshot. Have you been drinking?"*

The man gets really indignant and says, *"Officer, I couldn't help but notice your eyes are glazed. Have you been eating doughnuts?"*

The Devil tells a salesman, *"Look, I can make you richer, more famous, and more successful than any salesman alive. In fact, I can make you the greatest salesman that ever lived."*

"Well," says the salesman, *"what do I have to do in return?"*

The Devil smiles, *"Well, of course you have to give me your soul,"* he says, *"but you also have to give me the souls of your children, the souls of your children's children and, as a matter of fact, you have to give me the souls of all your descendants throughout eternity."*

"Wait a minute," the salesman says cautiously, *"What's the catch?"*

A new client had just come in to see a famous lawyer.

"Can you tell me how much you charge?" said the client.

"Of course," the lawyer replied, *"I charge $200 to answer three questions!"*

"Well that's a bit steep, isn't it?"

"Yes it is," said the lawyer, *"And what's your third question?"*

✳ **A** man walks into a New York City bank and says he wants to borrow $2,000 for three weeks. The loan officer asks him what kind of collateral he has. The man says *"I've got a Rolls Royce -- keep it until the loan is paid off -- here are the keys."* The loan officer promptly has the car driven into the bank's underground parking for safe keeping, and gives the man $2,000.

Three weeks later the man comes into the bank, pays back the $2,000 loan, plus $10 interest, and regains possession of the Rolls Royce. The loan officer asks him, *"Sir, if I may ask, why would a man who drives a Rolls Royce need to borrow $2,000?"*

The man answers, *"I had to go to Europe for three weeks, and where else could I store a Rolls Royce for that long for ten dollars?"*

❗ **T**he only reason a great many American families don't own an elephant is that they have never been offered an elephant for a dollar down and easy weekly payments. ~ *Mad Magazine.*

☯ **W**ives, you know you're married to a real football addict if he refers to you as his first-round draft choice.

A police officer pulls over this guy who had been weaving in and out of the lanes. He goes up to the guy's window and says *"Sir, I need you to blow into this breathalyzer tube."*

The man says, *"Sorry officer I can't do that. I am an asthmatic. If I do that I'll have a really bad asthma attack."*

"Okay, fine. I need you to come down to the station to give a blood sample."

"I can't do that either. I am a hemophiliac. If I do that, I'll bleed to death."

"Well, then we need a urine sample."

"I'm sorry officer I can't do that either. I am also a diabetic. If I do that I'll get really low blood sugar."

"Alright then I need you to come out here and walk this white line."

"I can't do that, officer."

"Why not?"

"Because I'm too drunk."

If you want to keep your teeth in good condition, brush your teeth after every meal and mind your own business.

♟ **H**ow do competing salespeople usually greet each other?

"Hi. Nice to meet you. I'm better than you."

☯ **A**ny married man should forget his mistakes, there's no use in two people remembering the same thing.

♟ **H**ow many salespeople does it take to change a light bulb?

None. *"You don't need a new light bulb - you need to upgrade your socket to the newest version."*

Just one, but it'll take technical support weeks to sort out the mess left behind.

Four. One to change the bulb and three to pull the chair out from under him.

✚ **I** asked my doctor, *"Doc, what can you do for me for $50?"*

He said, *"I'll send you a get well card."*

! **T**he Dictionary: What hi-tech salespeople say and what they mean by it.

New: Different color from previous design.

All new: Parts not interchangable with previous design.

Unmatched: Almost as good as the competition.

Designed simplicity: Manufacturer's cost cut to the bone.

Foolproof operation: No provision for adjustments.

Advanced design: The advertising agency doesn't understand it.

Field-tested: Manufacturer lacks test equipment.

High accuracy: Unit on which all parts fit.

Direct sales only: Factory had big argument with distributor.

Years of development: We finally got one that works.

Revolutionary: It's different from our competitiors.

Breakthrough: We finally figured out a way to sell it.

Improved: Didn't work the first time.

Futuristic: No other reason why it looks the way it does.

Distinctive: A different shape and color than the others.

Re-designed: Previous faults corrected, we hope.

Performance proven: Will operate through the warranty period.

Meets all standards: Ours, not yours.

Broadcast quality: Gives a picture and produces noise.

High reliability: We made it work long enough to ship it.

New generation: Old design failed, maybe this one will work.

Customer service across the country: You can return it from most airports.

Unprecedented performance: Nothing we ever had before worked this way.

Built to precision tolerances: We finally got it to fit together.

Microprocessor controlled: Does things we can't explain.

Latest aerospace technology: One of our techs was laid off by Boeing.

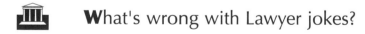 **W**hat's wrong with Lawyer jokes?

Lawyers don't think they're funny, and nobody else thinks they're jokes.

❋ You know our football team was so bad that one Saturday we tore down the goal posts hoping that would keep our team from playing the next week.

A worker who was being paid by the week approached his employer and held up his last paycheck. *"This is two hundred dollars less than we agreed on,"* he said.

"I know," the employer said. *"But last week I overpaid you two hundred dollars, and you never complained."*

"Well, I don't mind an occasional mistake," the worker answered, *"but when it gets to be a habit, I feel I have to call it to your attention."*

☺ A teacher was having trouble teaching arithmetic to one little boy. So she said, *"If you reached in your right pocket and found a nickel, and you reached in your left pocket and found another one, what would you have?"*

He replied, *"Somebody else's pants.*

✳ **A** traveler became lost in the Sahara desert. Realizing his only chance for survival was to find civilization, he began walking. Time passed, and he became thirsty. More time passed, and he began feeling faint. He was on the verge of passing out when he spied a tent about 500 meters in front of him. Barely conscious, he reached the tent and called out, *"Water."*

A bedouin appeared in the tent door and replied sympathetically, *"I am sorry, sir, but I have no water. However, would you like to buy a tie?"* With this, he brandished a collection of exquisite silken neckwear.

"You fool," gasped the man. *"I'm dying! I need water!"*

"Well, sir," replied the bedouin, *"If you really need water, there is a tent about two kilometers south of here where you can get some."*

Without knowing how, the man summoned sufficient strength to drag his parched body the distance to the second tent. With his last ounce of strength he tugged at the door of the tent and collapsed.

Another bedouin, dressed in a costly tuxedo, appeared at the door and enquired, *"May I help you sir?"*

"Water," was the feeble reply.

"Oh, sir," replied the bedouin, *"I'm sorry, but you can't come in here without a tie!"*

An airliner was having engine trouble, and the pilot instructed the cabin crew to have the passengers take their seats and get prepared for an emergency landing.

A few minutes later, the pilot asked the flight attendants if everyone was buckled in and ready.

"All set back here, Captain," came the reply, *"except one lawyer who is still going around passing out business cards."*

A police officer stopped a motorist who was speeding down Main Street. *"But officer,"* the man began, *"I can explain."*

"Just be quiet," snapped the officer. *"I'm going to let you cool your heels in jail until the chief gets back."*

"But, officer, I just wanted to say,"

"And I said to keep quiet! You're going to jail!"

A few hours later the officer looked in on his prisoner and said, *"Lucky for you that the chief's at his daughter's wedding. He'll be in a good mood when he gets back."*

"Don't count on it," answered the fellow in the cell. *"I'm the groom."*

✳ **A**n unemployed guy got a new job at the zoo. He was to dress up in a gorilla's skin and pretend to be a gorilla so people would keep coming to the zoo.

On his first day on the job, the guy puts on the skin and goes into the cage. The people all cheer to see him. He starts really putting on a show, jumping around, beating his chest and roaring.

During one acrobatic attempt, though, he lost his balance and crashed through some safety netting, landing square in the middle of the lion cage! As he lay there stunned, the lion roars. He's terrified and starts screaming, *"Help, Help!"*

The lion races over to him, places his paws on his chest and hisses, *"Shut up or we'll both lose our jobs!"*

🏛 **A** man died and was taken to his place of eternal torment by the devil. As he passed sulfurous pits and shrieking sinners, he saw a man he recognized as a lawyer snuggling up to a beautiful woman.

"That's unfair!" he cried. *"I have to roast for all eternity, and that lawyer gets to spend it with a beautiful woman."*

"Shut up!" barked the devil, jabbing him with his pitchfork. *"Who are you to question that woman's punishment?"*

The local sheriff was looking for a deputy, so Gomer went in to try out for the job.

"Okay," the sheriff drawled, *"Gomer, what is 1 and 1?"*

"11," he replied.

The sheriff thought to himself, *"That's not what I meant, but he's right."*

"What two days of the week start with the letter 'T'?"

"Today and tomorrow."

The sheriff was again surprised that Gomer supplied a correct answer that he had never thought of himself.

"Now Gomer, listen carefully. Who killed Abraham Lincoln?"

Gomer looked a little surprised, then thought really hard for a minute and finally admitted, *"I don't know."*

"Well, why don't you go home and work on that one for a while?"

So, Gomer wandered over to the barbershop where his pals were waiting to hear the results of the interview. Gomer was exultant. *"It went great! First day on the job and I'm already working on a murder case!"*

A miserly old man was on his death bed. He wanted badly to take his money with him. He called his priest, his doctor and his lawyer to his bedside. *"Here's $30,000 cash to be held by each of you. I trust you to put this in my coffin when I die so I can take all my money with me."*

At the funeral, each man put an envelope in the coffin. Riding away in a limousine, the priest suddenly broke into tears and confessed, *"I only put $20,000 into the envelope because I needed $10,000 for a new baptistery."*

"Well, since we're confiding in each other," said the doctor, *"I only put $10,000 in the envelope because we needed a new machine at the hospital which cost $20,000."*

The lawyer was aghast. *"I'm ashamed of both of you,"* he exclaimed. *"I want it known that when I put my envelope in that coffin, it held my personal check for the full $30,000."*

✚ **A**n applicant was being interviewed for admission to a prominent medical school. *"Tell me,"* inquired the interviewer, *"where do you expect to be ten years from now?"*

"Well, let's see," replied the student. *"It's Wednesday afternoon. I guess I'll be on the golf course."*

A woman and her little girl were visitng the grave of the little girl's grandmother. On their way through the cemetery back to the car, the little girl asked, *"Mommy, do they ever bury two people in the same grave?"*

"Of course not, dear," replied the mother, *"why would you think that?"*

"The tombstone back there said 'Here lies a lawyer and an honest man.'"

The boss arrived at the office early one morning and found an employee kissing his secretary. *"Young man,"* he said, *"is this what I pay you for?"*

The young man replied, *"No, sir, this I do for free."*

A waiter brings the customer the steak he ordered with his thumb over the meat.

"Are you crazy?" yelled the customer, *"You have your hand on my steak!"*

"What," answers the waiter, *"do you want it to fall on the floor again?"*

! Several weeks after a young man had been hired, he was called into the personnel manager's office.

"What is the meaning of this?" the manager asked. *"When you applied for the job, you told us you had 5 years' experience. Now, we discover this is the first job you've ever had."*

"Well," the young man said, *"in your ad you said you wanted somebody with imagination."*

When a visitor to a small town in Georgia came upon a wild dog attacking a young boy, he quickly grabbed the animal and throttled it with his two hands.

A reporter saw the incident, congratulated the man and told him the headline the following day would read, *"Valiant Local Man Saves Child by Killing Vicious Animal."*

The hero told the journalist that he wasn't from that town.

"Well, then," the reporter said, "the headline will probably say, *'Georgia Man Saves Child by Killing Dog.'"*

"Actually," the man said, *"I'm from Connecticut."*

"In that case," the reporter said in a huff, *"the headline should read, 'Yankee Kills Family Pet.'"*

A business was looking for office help. They put a sign in the window, stating the following:

HELP WANTED

Must be able to type, have computer skills, and be bilingual. We are an Equal Opportunity Employer.

A dog trotted up to the window, saw the sign and went inside. He looked at the receptionist and wagged his tail, then walked over to the sign, looked at it and whined a bit.

Getting the idea, the receptionist got the office manager. The office manager looked at the dog and was surprised, to say the least. However, the dog looked determined, so he led him into the office. Inside, the dog jumped up on a chair and stared at the manager. The manager said, *"I can't hire you. The sign says you have to be able to type."*

The dog jumped down, went to the typewriter and proceeded to type out a perfect letter. He took out the page and trotted over to the manager and gave it to him, then jumped back up on the chair. The manager was stunned, but then told the dog, *"The sign also says you have to be good with a computer."*

The dog jumped down again and went to the computer. The dog proceeded to enter and execute a perfect spreadsheet that worked flawlessly the first time.

By this time, the manager was totally dumb-founded! He looked at the dog and said, *"I realize that you are a very intelligent dog and have some interesting abilities. However, I still can't give you the job."*

The dog jumped down and went over to a copy of the sign and put his paw on the sentence about being an Equal Opportunity Employer.

The manager said, *"Yes, but the sign also says that you have to be bilingual."*

The dog looked straight at that manager and said, *"Mcow."*

☀ **A** man goes into a drugstore and asks the pharmacist if he can give him something for the hiccups. The pharmacist promptly reaches out and slaps the man's face.

"What did you do that for?" the man asks.

"Well, you don't have the hiccups anymore, do you?"

The man says, *"No, but my wife out in the car still does!"*

☯ **I** just got back from a pleasure trip. I took my mother-in-law to the airport.

🕷 How to Give a Cat a Pill

1. Pick up cat and cradle it in the crook of your left arm as if holding a baby. Position right fore-finger and thumb on either side of cat's mouth and gently apply pressure to cheeks while hold-ing pill in right hand. As cat opens mouth, pop pill into mouth. Allow cat to close mouth and swallow.

2. Retrieve pill from floor and cat from behind sofa. Cradle cat in left arm and repeat process.

3. Retrieve cat from bedroom and throw soggy pill away.

4. Take new pill from foil wrap, cradle cat in left arm holding rear paws tightly with left hand. Force jaws open and push pill to back of mouth with right forefinger. Hold mouth shut for count of ten.

5. Retrieve pill from goldfish bowl and cat from top of wardrobe. Call spouse from garden.

6. Kneel on floor with cat wedged firmly between knees, hold front and rear paws. Ignore low growls emitted by cat. Get spouse to hold head firmly down and rub cat's throat vigorously.

7. Retrieve cat from curtain rail, and get another pill from foil wrap. Make note to repair curtains. Carefully sweep shattered figurines and vases from hearth and set to one side for gluing later.

8. Wrap cat in large towel and get spouse to lie on cat with head just visible from below armpit. Put pill in end of drinking straw, force mouth open with pencil and blow down drinking straw.

9. Check label to make sure pill not harmful to human. Drink 1 beer to take taste away. Apply bandage to spouse's forearm and remove blood from carpet with cold water.

10. Retrieve cat from neighbor's shed. Get another pill. Open another beer. Place cat in cupboard and close door gently onto neck, leaving head showing. Force mouth open with dessert spoon. Flick pill down throat with elastic band.

11. Fetch screwdriver from garage and put cupboard door back on hinges. Drink beer. Fetch bottle of scotch. Pour shot, drink. Apply cold compress to cheek and check records for date of last tetanus shot. Apply whiskey compress to cheek to disinfect. Toss back another shot. Throw torn and bloody T-shirt away and fetch new one from bedroom.

12. Call fire department to retrieve cat from tree across the road. Apologize to neighbor who crashed into fence while swerving to avoid cat. Take last pill from foil wrap.

13. Tie the little creep's front paws to rear paws with garden twine and bind tightly to leg of dining table, find heavy-duty pruning gloves from shed. Push pill into mouth followed by large piece of steak. Hold cat's head vertically

and pour 2 pints of water down throat to wash pill down.

14. Consume remainder of scotch. Get spouse to drive you to the emergency room. Sit quietly while doctor stitches fingers and forearm and removes pill remnants from right eye. Call furniture shop on way home to order new table.

15. Arrange for SPCA to collect mutant cat and call local pet shop to see if they have any hamsters.

How to Give a Dog a Pill

1. Wrap it in bacon.

2. Toss it in the air.

❗ **A** manager of a retail clothing store is reviewing a potential employee's application and notices that the man has never worked in retail before. He says to the man, *"For a man with no experience, you are certainly asking for a high wage."*

"Well sir," the applicant replies, *"the work is so much harder when you don't know what you're doing!"*

✳ **T**he doorbell rang and the lady of the house discovered a workman, complete with tool chest, on the front porch. *"Madam,"* he announced, *"I'm the piano tuner."*

The lady exclaimed, *"Why, I didn't send for a piano tuner."*

The man replied, *"I know you didn't, but your neighbors did."*

❦ **A** newsboy was standing on the corner with a stack of papers, yelling, *"Read all about it. Fifty people swindled! Fifty people swindled!"*

Curious, a man walked over, bought a paper, and checked the front page. Finding nothing, the man said, *"There's nothing in here about fifty people being swindled."*

The newsboy ignored him and went on, calling out, *"Read all about it. Fifty-one people swindled!"*

✳ **W**hat's the difference between a taxidermist and a tax collector?

The taxidermist only takes the skin.

☺   Teacher to student: *"Did you write this poem by yourself?"*

"Of course," said the young student, *"Every word of it."*

"Well, I am very glad to meet you, Mr. Edgar Allan Poe, I had heard you were dead."

❗   Shopkeeper Smith was alarmed when a new business, much like his own, opened in the storefront to the left of him. A huge sign was installed, reading BEST DEALS.

Mr. Smith was troubled a second time when another competitor leased the building on his right, and erected a much larger sign, reading LOWEST PRICES.

At this point Smith was really depressed, however, he came up with an idea. He put the biggest sign of all over his own shop. It read MAIN ENTRANCE.

☺   Little Tommy went to his dad and said, *"Dad, can you write in the dark?"*

"I think so. What is it you want me to write?"

"Your name on this report card."

! **A** guy calls a law firm by the name of Schwartz, Schwartz, Schwartz and Schwartz, and he asks, *"Is Mr. Schwartz there?"*

The guy answering the phone says, *"No, Mr. Schwartz is in Palm Beach."*

So he asks, *"Well, is Mr. Schwartz there?"* and the guy says, *"No, Mr. Schwartz is playing golf."*

So he asks, *"Well what about Mr. Schwartz?"* And the guy says, *"No, he's at a law convention in Las Vegas."*

So he says, *"Well, what about Mr. Schwartz?"* And the guy says, *"Speaking."*

✻ **D**ispatcher: *"9-1-1 What's the nature of your emergency?"*

Caller: *"My wife is pregnant, and her contractions are only two minutes apart."*

Dispatcher: *"Is this her first child?"*

Caller: *"No, you idiot! This is her husband!"*

☯ **Y**ou know, she's a terrible cook. She's so bad that we pray after we eat.

! The manager of a large office noticed a new man one day and told him to come into his office. *"What is your name?"* was the first thing the manager asked him.

"John," the new guy replied.

The manager scowled, *"Look, I don't know what kind of a namby-pamby place you worked at before, but I don't call anyone by their first name. It breeds familiarity and that leads to a breakdown in authority. I refer to my employees by their last name only - Smith, Jones, Baker - that's all. I am to be referred to only as Mr. Robertson. Now that we got that straight, what is your last name?"*

The new guy sighed and said, *"Darling. My name is John Darling."*

"Okay, John, the next thing I want to tell you is..."

☺ **A** little girl came home from school and said to her mother, *"Mommy, today in school I was punished for something that I didn't do."*

The mother exclaimed, *"But that's terrible! I'm going to have a talk with your teacher about this. By the way, what was it that you didn't do?"*

The little girl replied, *"My homework."*

Employee's Ten Commandments

If at first you don't succeed, destroy all evidence that you tried.

If you can't get your work done in the first 24 hours, work nights.

Experience is something you don't get until just after you need it.

For every action, there is an equal and opposite criticism.

Keep your boss's boss off your boss's back.

Success always occurs in private, and failure in full view.

To steal ideas from one person is plagiarism; to steal from many is research.

The sooner you fall behind, the more time you'll have to catch up.

Don't be irreplaceable, if you can't be replaced, you can't be promoted.

If you are good, you will be assigned all the work. If you are really good, you will get out of it.

What a golfer! The other day, he missed a hole in one by only four strokes.

◯ **A**fter watching sales falling off for three straight months at Kentucky Fried Chicken, the Colonel calls up the Pope and asks for a favor.

The Pope says, *"What can I do?"*

The Colonel says, *"I need you to change the daily prayer from, 'Give us this day our daily bread' to 'Give us this day our daily chicken.' If you do it, I'll donate $10 million to the Vatican."*

The Pope replies, *"I am sorry. That is the Lord's prayer and I can not change the words."* So the Colonel hangs up.

After another month of dismal sales, the Colonel panics, and calls again. *"Listen, your Excellency. I really need your help. I'll donate $50 million dollars if you change the words of the daily prayer from 'Give us this day our daily bread' to 'Give us this day our daily chicken.'"*

And the Pope responds, *"It is very tempting, Colonel Sanders. The church could do a lot of good with that much money. It would help us to support many charities. But, again, I must decline. It is the Lord's prayer, and I can't change the words."*

So the Colonel gives up again. After two more months of terrible sales. The Colonel gets desperate. *"This is my final offer, your Excellency. If you change the words of the daily prayer from, 'Give us this day our daily bread' to 'Give us this day our daily chicken' I will donate $100 million to the Vatican."*

The Pope replies, *"Let me get back to you."*

So the next day, the Pope calls together all of his cardinals and he says, *"I have some good news and I have some bad news. The good news is that KFC is going to donate $100 million to the Vatican."*

The bishops rejoice at the news. Then one asks about the bad news. The Pope replies, "*The bad news is that we lost the Wonder Bread account.*"

! **A** young man, hired by a supermarket, reported for his first day of work. The manager greeted him with a warm handshake and a smile, gave him a broom and said, *"Your first job will be to sweep out the store."*

"But I'm a college graduate," the young man replied indignantly.

"Oh, I'm sorry. I didn't realize that," said the manager. *"Here, give me the broom, I'll show you how."*

✚ **H**e was an honest doctor. On the death certificate, where it said "cause of death" he signed his name.

A big company offered $50 for each money-saving idea submitted by its employees. First prize went to the employee who suggested the award be cut to $25.

An older gentleman approached a young lady and asked, *"Where have you been all my life?"*

She answered, *"Well, for the first 40 years, I wasn't even born."*

Employer to applicant: *"Where did you get your training?"*

"Yale."

"Good, and what's your name?"

"Yim Yohnson."

How many folk musicians does it take to change a light bulb?

Seven; one to change and the other six to sing about how good the old one was.

❗ *"**I** have to have a raise,"* the man said to his boss. *"There are three other companies after me."*

"Is that so?" asked the manager. *"What other companies are after you?"*

"The electric company, the telephone company, and the gas company."

✚ A doctor is to give a speech at the local AMA dinner. He jots down notes for his speech. Unfortunately, when he stands in front of his colleagues later that night, he finds that he can't read his notes. So he asks, *"Is there a pharmacist in the house?"*

☯ **A** man and his wife were sitting in the living room and he said to her, *"Just so you know, I never want to live in a vegetative state, dependent on some machine and fluids from a bottle. If that ever happens, just pull the plug."*

His wife got up, unplugged the TV and threw out all of his beer.

About Ben Brooks

Ben Brooks loves to laugh and to make people laugh. He really enjoys hearing a good joke and likes telling one even more. And, Ben has a lot to smile about because he is the unchallenged leader in investing in and developing real estate opportunities and has helped thousands of investors attain tremendous success, security, pride of ownership and profits. However, Ben's life was not always one of laughter and success. In fact, he had a very rough childhood and young adulthood.

Ben's parents divorced when Ben and his sister were still quite young so they grew up without a father figure. Ben had to be the "man" of the house, so he started working in grade school and continued to work hard throughout high school to support his mother, sister and brother. Due to his circumstances, Ben never gave college any serious consideration. When he got his real estate license at 19, Ben felt that he was finally on his way.

Although Ben always loved hearing a good joke, he started telling them when he found himself in awkward situations. Ben admits he lacked self-confidence because he felt he did not have the same level of education as many of his friends and business peers. Therefore, to mask his lack of education, he would divert the conversation by telling a joke and getting a laugh.

Ben got married when he was 21, and had his son, 'Tres" a year later. Ben and his family moved to Arizona in 1963 after being offered a sales manager position for a real estate company. He had never sold real estate but accepted the job and moved. After settling in Arizona, the Brooks were blessed with the birth of their daughter, Julie.

Ben did get an education in real estate but it was through the "school of hard knocks." He worked many different jobs throughout the beginning of his real estate career and each one taught him another facet of the industry. All the while, he continued telling jokes and tales and making friends, family and customers laugh.

Ben founded Ben Brooks & Associates in 1969 and currently serves as Chairman and CEO of the company. The company is a full-service real estate company specializing in acquiring and developing land in the Southwest. Ben's company has purchased, developed and marketed over one million acres of land throughout its history. Now Ben truly has something to smile about!

Ben has played an integral role in many local Arizona communities. He is a former Realtor of the Year and past President of the Scottsdale Board of Realtors. He has served in executive positions and on boards of numerous civic, business, and charitable organizations including Arizona Association of Realtors, the Young President's Organizations (YPO), Phoenix Thunderbirds, Sun West Development Corporation, a state chartered bank, a publicly traded restaurant chain and the globally recognized Barrow Neurological Institute.

Ben is currently a member of the prestigious World President's Organization (WPO), a graduate of the Federal Bureau of Investigations (FBI) Citizens Academy, the past Colonel/Commander of the Maricopa Sheriff's Advisory Posse, and a member of the Executive Committee of the Maricopa County Sheriff's Office's Memorial Fund. He is also a member of the Forest Highlands, Paradise Valley and Phoenix Country Clubs.

Although he is a very successful businessman, Ben still has memories of his difficult childhood. Although he knows that being opportunistic along with his drive and intelligence were the major factors to his success, he believes that his ability to tell jokes, comical tales and stories have also played an important role in his life.

Ben has collected jokes for the past 20+ years and is thrilled to work with his cherished friend, Tom Hopkins, in compiling some of his and Tom's favorites into their first book.

About Tom Hopkins

Tom Hopkins is a master sales trainer. He has helped over three million sales professionals around the world to understand how to better serve their clients. He has fought long and hard to shatter the old stereotype of selling that people who go into sales as a career are pushy and aggressive.

Although he was only 19 years old, Tom got his start in sales in the real estate industry in Southern California. At the time, real estate was considered an "old man's" profession. The only suit he owned was his high school band uniform and his vehicle was a motorcycle. You had to have a sense of humor to even attempt to sell real estate under those circumstances.

His first six months in real estate, Tom didn't do well, only moving one property. He was down to his last $150 in savings and invested it in a three-day sales training course with J. Douglas Edwards, who was renowned as the Father of American Selling. Taking copious notes and studying all hours of the night, Tom took home the award of top student and his whole life began to turn around.

Tom went on to achieve levels of success in real estate that were previously unheard of. He closed 1,553 transactions in 6 years--365 of which were in a single year. Tom was genuinely interested in the welfare of his clients and learned to put them at ease with humor.

As the recipient of many sales awards, Tom was asked to give acceptance speeches. While he had become extremely successful in sales...working with clients one-on-one, Tom had an overwhelming fear of public speaking.

Fortunately, J. Douglas Edwards had been following Tom's phenomenal career and began mentoring him. He told Tom to "do what you fear most and you will conquer fear." So, Tom began working to become more proficient at public speaking. Once again, he used the power of humor in his speeches to win over his audiences.

Over and over again, others who heard him speak would want

to talk with Tom after his speech to learn how he had achieved such a phenomenal selling career. Tom began to incorporate some of his strategies and tactics into his speeches. Seeing the light of understanding dawn on the faces of those in attendance helped Tom realize that training others would become his lifelong passion. He didn't want others to have to struggle as he did early on.

When Tom started his new life as a sales and motivational trainer, he moved to Arizona from California. At one of his first teaching presentations for the Phoenix Board of Realtors, Tom met one of the most charming, delightful and fun people he had ever known--Ben Brooks. That first meeting set the stage for a lifelong friendship. Both men are passionate about serving others while enjoying themselves along the way.

Tom Hopkins International was established in 1976 with a goal of providing solid, how-to sales training to anyone who chooses the profession of selling as their career. Training is provided via seminars, video, in print and audio formats. Over three million sales professionals on five continents have benefited from Tom Hopkins training. Tom is the author of twelve books on the subjects of selling and self-motivation. His books have sold millions of copies worldwide and continue to be in great demand today.

Tom and Ben have shared the joys and endured the challenges life brings over 30-plus years of friendship with caring hearts and tons of laughs...understanding that as long as you can keep your sense of humor, you can survive anything.

It's with great honor that Tom is co-authoring a book with his good friend, Gentle Ben. His goal is to bring joy, happiness and great prosperity to those who indulge themselves in laughter for both health and wealth!

JOKE INDEX